The Alternative Advent Calendar

SECRETS OF THE TRUE SPIRIT OF CHRISTMAS

The Alternative Advent Calendar:
Secrets of the True Spirit of Christmas

© 2019 Gillian Monks

The moral rights of the author have been asserted.

All rights reserved. No part of this publication may be reproduced, distributed, or transmitted in any form or by any means, including photocopying, recording, or other electronic or mechanical methods, without the prior written permission of the publisher, except in the case of brief quotations embodied in critical reviews and certain other non-commercial uses permitted by copyright law. For permission requests, write to the publisher at the email address below.

The author welcomes relevant correspondence and questions: gillian@gillianmonks.com

First Edition, 2019.

Published by Herbary Books
Caernarfon, Wales

Typeset in St. Nicholas.

ISBN 978-1-5272-4942-4

Printed & Distributed by IngramSpark.

Dedication

To John and Annie,
Without who's constant love, support, suggestions and ideas this book would have been all the poorer, and my task much harder.

My thanks and love... always.

Contents

Doors to Open

Introduction	1
Advent and the Advent Calendar	3
Ideas For Alternative Advent Calendars	10
Door 1: Give everyone you see today a smile	16
Door 2: Light a candle in the darkness	20
Door 3: Spend some quality time with someone	24
Door 4: Make someone a hot drink	28
Door 5: Play the part of Saint Nicholas	32
Door 6: Sing a Christmas carol	36
Door 7: Write a seasonal card to a neighbour	40
Door 8: Give yourself the gift of freedom	44
Door 9: Give Christmas hugs to everyone	48
Door 10: Feed the birds	52
Door 11: Leave a message of loving kindness	56
Door 12: Phone or message a friend	60

Door 13: Give thankfulness and gratitude	64
Door 14: Speak kindly to something in the natural world	68
Door 15: Give the gift of a good temper	72
Door 16: Give a Christmas stocking	76
Door 17: Make people laugh	80
Door 18: Share a living gift	84
Door 19: Tell someone you love them	88
Door 20: Extend the hand of friendship	92
Door 21: Sow some seeds	96
Door 22: Offer deep appreciation	100
Door 23: Bless your home	104
Door 24: Celebrate Mother's Night	108
Door 25: The extra door	112
What next?	116
Acknowledgements	121

Introduction

The Alternative Advent Calendar Explained

With the publication of my first book, 'Merry Midwinter; How to Rediscover the Magic of the Christmas Season' in October 2018, I was keen to continue to expand the whole idea of giving gifts with a difference. The 'Alternative Advent Calendar' originally came into being as twenty-five posts on my Merry Midwinter blog.

However once Christmas Day had been reached, it seemed such a shame to simply abandon it. I decided to rewrite it in a more considered and thoughtful form to offer to a wider audience of readers.

This advent calendar in book form will not show you pretty pictures or give you indulgences to eat. The 'Alternative Advent Calendar' is not about what pleasure it can bring you but what you can do for others - although I sincerely hope that it will also bring you enormous pleasure too. Midwinter has always been a time of giving of oneself, of service to others and a literal celebration of peace, even in times of war.

Weary, jaded and disillusioned by all the false pressures of commercialisation and consumerism which surround our modern celebration of Midwinter and Christmas? Take heart, this advent calendar offers you the opportunity to do something else for a change. It encourages you to take control of your life and do something of real practical value and use, suggesting ways in which you can begin to integrate your more loving, caring, concerned impulses and nature into actions which will bring comfort, courage and joy. No money is necessarily involved. You don't have to be financially wealthy. You are already rich beyond your wildest dreams in what you contain within yourself - endless potential!

You do, however, need to have a willingness to reach out to the world around you - to walk your talk... or even decide what your 'talk' actually entails.

The ideas, simple tasks and challenges this book suggests to you are universally relevant, regardless of geographical and genetic origins, social, academic or professional status, cultural background, religion or belief. They are basic actions which are applicable to anyone anywhere in the world. They are something to offer of yourself - a kindness, some of your time, thought, care, appreciation... a different focus for every day between the first and the twenty-fifth of December. Nor are these 'tasks' particularly out of the ordinary - they are designed to slot into your everyday life, schedules and pre-Christmas preparations and activities. Simple. Accessible. A few are related to the time of year and season but can easily be reapplied to any time of year.

If you are given this little book as a Christmas present, why not wait and decide to follow it through January instead? Take a look at the back of the book under the section headed "What Happens After Christmas?" for more ideas about doing this.

Come with me and have a look each day - open each Advent 'door' to find out what you are asked to do next - and by the time the Sun rises on Christmas morning, your attitude to life might have radically changed and you may discover your very own magical Christmas gift!

Lastly, however you decide to use these simple suggestions, remember to enjoy yourself too. You aren't going to do any good at all if you allow yourself to become a sanctimonious 'do-gooder'. As a very gentle, elderly Quaker lady used to love to tell me when I was just a slip of a teenager, "The Lord doth love a merry heart!"

My wish for you, dear reader, is that this Advent - and all the months to follow - be filled with new adventures, experiences and achievements.

Have a wonderfully adventurous 'Alternative Advent'.

With my love.
~ Gillian Monks,   North Wales, 2019.

Advent & the Advent Calendar

What & When is Advent?

Originally there was no particular connection between Advent and Christmas. In the Christian church Advent, like Lent, was a forty-day period of repentance and fasting during which Christian converts studied in preparation for being baptized. The observation of Advent taking place directly before Christmas seems to have begun in Gaul (modern day France) during the Fourth Century A.D., although there are many other theories sited as to where and when it was first observed.

The Gallic fast began at sundown after the celebration of the Feast of Martin of Tours on the 11th November. Martin was a Roman cavalry officer who became a Christian and founded the first monastery in Gaul. Interestingly, this was traditionally the date when herds of animals were culled before the ravages of the winter weather. Even more interestingly, forty days on from the 11th November brings us, not to the 24th December and Christmas Eve, but to the 20th December and the eve of the Winter Solstice. As Gaul, (like the British Isles and other areas of western Europe), had long been an area of Druidic practice, perhaps this is not so surprising.

A similar three - six week period of fasting was observed in Rome and this was eventually combined with the Gallic observance and later adopted by the Eastern Sees making it fairly universally followed - unsurprisingly with one difference, the beginning of this forty day Advent had been moved to sunset on the 14th November so that it by-passed the Solar celebration and did indeed end on Christmas Eve.

The meaning of the word Advent is derived from the Latin word *adventus* which means 'coming' or 'arrival'. It was first used to translate the Greek word *Parousia* which actually refers to the Second Coming of Christ 'in clouds to judge the world' and not at all to do with the birth of a baby in a stable in Bethlehem.

These days the western Christian Catholic and Protestant churches celebrate the period of Advent over the course of the last four Sundays before Christmas Day, with the First Sunday of Advent falling somewhere between the last few days in November and the first three days in December. Advent is now more commonly associated with the anticipation of the anniversary of Christ's birth, a time of spiritual reflection and preparation, a season of waiting.

The Advent Wreath & Candles

It isn't known exactly where or when the practice of making an Advent wreath originated. Some sources maintain that the practice dates from the early 19th Century but this cannot be correct. In the 18th Century the Lutheran Churches in Scandinavia used to place twenty-four small candles around the rim of a wooden wheel and light one for every day of the twenty-four days of Advent throughout December.

The Advent wreath as we know it now is something that is found both in places of Christian worship and in family homes. It is formed from a circle of evergreens - representing eternal and never-ending life - in which four coloured candles are equally placed around a circle, with an optional fifth candle being stood in the centre. The first candle is lit on the first Sunday, followed by the second (and first) candle being lit on the second

Sunday of Advent until the fourth Sunday is reached when all four candles are lit and the light is (almost) at its brightest - depicting the increasing closeness to the return of the Light.

In this case, the Light is spiritual; celebrating the birth of Jesus Christ who has been called 'The Light of The World' because he brought the message of how vital unconditional love is to us all - he was an enlightened prophet preaching a very modern and enlightened message.

It also refers to the return, or rebirth, of the Sun at Midwinter, the solar event of the Winter Solstice, when we experience the shortest, darkest day on the 21st December, and when we in the Northern Hemisphere are leaning furthest away from the warmth and light of the Sun. After the 21st December, the earth begins to tilt its northern half closer towards the Sun again and so our days begin to grow longer, lighter and warmer. But it is only on the morning of the 25th December (Christmas Day) that we are able to actually measure the increased amount of daylight.

Therefore it can be said that the Light/light of the Son/Sun is born/reborn at Midwinter, and exactly on the morning of the 25th. Hence the lighting of the Advent candles represents the approaching return of the 'light', however you care to interpret it.

Each candle has its own relevance and meaning.

The first candle to be lit, standing at the lower left (or eight o'clock position) of the circle, is purple or blue in colour and represents Isaiah and the other prophets in the Bible who predicted the coming of Jesus - it also stands for hope or promise.

The second candle to be lit stands at the top left (or ten o'clock position) of the circle is also purple or blue in colour and represents the Bible, waiting and prophecy - and more importantly, love.

The third candle to be lit at the top right (or two o'clock position) of the circle is rose pink in colour and represents the feminine (in this case, Mary, the mother of Jesus) and joy and peace.

The fourth candle to be lit stands at the bottom right (or four o'clock position) of the circle and is also purple or dark blue in colour. It represents love, peace and adoration and features John the Baptist, Jesus' cousin, who told the people of Israel to prepare for Jesus' teaching.

There can be a fifth candle which is stood in the centre of the circle formed by the wreath and which is white in colour and represents Jesus. In Germany it is called the *Heiligabend* and is lit on Christmas Eve; or it can be saved and lit on Christmas Day to celebrate that the Light has returned to the world.

Traditionally, the first two candles relate to the Second Coming of Christ... something to look forward to and prepare for in the future; while the second two candles relate to his first coming in the past and the beginning of the story with the Nativity.

In Protestant communities these different colours of candles are generally not recognised; in this instance all four candles around the wreath often all being red in colour but the central candle - if they have one - remains white.

A single Advent candle with the twenty-four days up to Christmas Day marked down the side of it became popular towards the end of the Twentieth Century. For this type of observance the candle is first lit on the 1st December and allowed to burn down to the first line, marking the first day of Advent. This is repeated every day; the candle being burnt down to the next succeeding line until the final line is reached on Christmas Eve. The remaining candle is lit on Christmas Day and allowed to completely burn away.

The Advent Calendar

Today the most common Advent calendar (certainly in the United Kingdom and the United States of America) is one made from paper or card with a large seasonally themed picture on the front depicting a snowy landscape, robins, wrens, stags or holly, Father Christmas, toys, a festively decorated home or a religious scene. In this picture are twenty-four numbered windows or doors, beginning on the 1st December and ending on the 24th December, Christmas Eve. One door is opened every day and a Christmas picture is displayed beneath.

The purpose of the Advent calendar is to increase the anticipation of Christmas and help to mark off the time left.

The History of the Advent Calendar

Like everything else, the origins of the Advent calendar are shrouded in uncertainty. In the 19th Century, German protestant Christians counted down the days to Christmas by marking twenty-four chalk lines on a door and then rubbing one off each day in December. It is believed that there was a relatively common practice among religious Lutheran families where little pictures were hung on the wall, one for each day of December. There is an early mention of an Advent calendar in a children's book by Elise Averdieck written in 1851 which tells of a mother telling the Christmas story and singing carols with her little daughter each evening and adding a new little picture to be pinned to the wall, until on Christmas Eve there were a whole collection of twenty-four illustrations.

The *Deutsche Weihnachtsmuseum* relates how the first Advent calendars were called 'Nicholas Calendars' and given out on the 6th December, Saint Nicholas' day. Later they began to run from the 1st December and were called 'Christmas Calendars' instead.

In 1902, a Christian bookshop in Hamburg published a Christmas Clock. This was a picture of a clock face divided into segments with a Christmas carol written in each segment. The Austrian *Landesmuseum* mentions that an Advent calendar was printed in 1903, and in 1904 an Advent calendar was inserted into the newspaper '*Neues Tagblatt Stuttgart*' as a gift for readers.

In 1908, Gerhard Lang, (born in Maulbronn, Germany in 1881) produced the first commercially printed Advent calendar. When he was a child, his mother made him twenty-four '*Wibbele*' (little candies) which were stuck to a piece of cardboard - or as others report, sewn into the lid of a box. As an adult, Lang became the participator of the printing office, 'Reichhold and Lang', where he had produced little coloured pictures which could be affixed to cardboard, one for every day of the month, up until the 24th December.

The popularity of these new Advent calendars grew and spread beyond the German border. Gerhard Lang also produced Advent trees and a type of Advent calendar which one had to actually break open to get at the contents. There was also an Advent house made from decorated cardboard which had twenty-four doors and windows around its four walls, each containing a transparent coloured paper covering each opening and then blocked by a cardboard covering or 'door'. A lighted candle was inserted into the house and starting on the 1st December, one door or window would be opened each night. The closer to Christmas, the greater the number of open windows and the greater the light, mimicking the 'growing light' which would be born/reborn on the morning of the 25th December, (whether as the culmination of the solar event of the Winter Solstice, the birth of any one of several mythical, archetypal figures or Jesus himself.)

The coming of World War II terminated the production of Advent calendars as paper was in short supply. After the war ended, Richard Sellmer produced the first commercial Advent calendar in 1946, emerging as the leading producer of seasonal cards and calendars and whose company is still in business today.

The early Advent calendars originally opened to reveal a part of a religious story or tract, a poem, Christmas picture or small gift. Advent calendars filled with chocolates first appeared in numbers in 1958 but only gained widespread popularity in the 1980's.

Now we have the most complicated and luxurious versions imaginable. From fabric pockets, sacks and bags to wooden drawers, boxes and cubby holes, the contents are as varied as our imaginations can make them:- sweets, chocolate, Lego and other toys for children; beauty products, socks, preserves and jams, stationary, vintage whiskeys and precious gems for the adults. The very essence of expensive, consumer-driven one-upmanship and overindulgence!

The Most Expensive...

In 2007, Harrods in London were selling an Advent calendar with a difference. It was a four-foot structure shaped like a Christmas Tree and carved from burr elm and walnut wood with each compartment containing organic chocolate. It had been made in aid of support for the cocoa farmers of Belize and sold for $50,000. But it was far from being the most expensive Advent calendar ever made. That accolade goes to a Belgian jeweller who, in 2010 made a glass calendar consisting of twenty-four glass tubes each containing diamonds and silver worth £2.1 million (2.5 million euros, $3.3 million)

The Largest...

According to the Guinness World Records the largest Advent calendar was built at St. Pancras railway station in London in 2007 to mark the re-opening of the station following renovation work. It measured 232feet, 11 inches tall and 75 feet and 5 inches wide.

Ideas for Alternative Advent Calendars

Today it is possible to buy an amazingly varied selection of Advent Calendars for all ages. There is no reason to stay with the concept of the Advent Calendar being one big picture which contains twenty-four doors behind which are concealed twenty-four little pictures. There is even less reason to buy the often garish or over-priced commercially produced versions on offer in the shops either.

Why not make your own? It needn't be based on pictures. Sew or glue together twenty-four little sacks or boots cut from material. Christmas colours of red, dark green, gold or silver or hessian to mimic Father Christmas's sack, or materials printed with holly or other seasonally themed illustrations can be very effective. Sew, paint or embroider a number on each boot or sack. With large tacking stitches, run a length of coloured embroidery thread around the top of each sack so that it can be drawn together at the top and tied to prevent anyone else seeing what might be hidden there. Or use a colourful ribbon or length of Christmas gift tie to secure the tops.

Place a tiny individual treat in each sack or boot which can be personally tailored to the tastes of the recipient. For children you might wish to include items with a practical use in the days and weeks before Christmas... things such as coloured pens, glitter, decorations to make and Christmas stickers. Hopefully, this will help to teach a child the true meaning of both Advent and Christmas - of anticipation and preparation and the giving of one's own time, thought and endeavour.

Or you might like to instigate an Advent treasure hunt. Buy or make twentyfour little containers (sacks, boots, socks, tiny packages, small envelopes... perhaps reuse last year's wooden calendar with drawers?) You might like to hang these from an Advent Tree - a small branch cut from the garden and set up in a plant pot of clean earth or sand. In each receptacle, place a clue as to where 'treasure' may be found. This can be just around the inside of the house or in the garden too. They might just be straightforward clues or they might be tasks like a game of forfeits; stand on one leg and sing the first verse of a carol, tell a joke, quak like a duck, tell everyone they are loved... you can be as imaginative and inventive as you like. (Also works well for all ages!)

For older children, teenagers and adults, the possibilities are endless. How about twenty-four inspiring seasonal quotations? Or twenty-four quotations based around a theme which interests the person you are going to give it to, such as gardening, history, cookery or animals. Or how about writing out a selection of family recipes? Or for the family history expert, twenty-four little stories, reminiscences or brief accounts of significant family events - this might be a really good one for an older member of the family to work on and a wonderful way for them to share their memories with a younger generation.

How about making a simple calendar for family or your workplace and providing a joke for each day, with everyone taking a turn to open it and read it out? People might wryly groan, but it is a good way to bring a burst of laughter to a group of people or place and can help to set the tone for the rest of the day. You could simply write the jokes out and place each one in its own numbered envelope pinned to a notice board.

When you have filled your sacks or boots - or whatever you choose to use as your containers - you can then hang them from a single length of coloured string or ribbon tied across the ceiling of a room or draped across a wall where they can be seen and anticipated.... but out of reach! Or you may prefer to make an 'Advent Tree' as previously described.

Another variation would be to find a cardboard box large enough to contain the twenty-four gifts you have assembled. Decorate the box with Christmas paper (or any other artistically inspired method). Cut twenty-four doors in the top and sides of the box and number them. Wrap your gifts (keep them as small as possible as they have to be able to pass through the doors you have cut) and tie a length of coloured string, wool or ribbon to each one. Place your gifts in the box. Carefully thread each end of string from a gift out through a door and secure on the outside with sticky tape so that it doesn't get dragged back into the box and lost. Finally, make sure all the little cardboard doors are closed and seal up the box. You can decorate the whole with fairy lights if you like. Let your imagination have free rein... and enjoy yourself! Just because you are making something for someone else doesn't mean that you shouldn't enjoy it too, especially as you might have to then sit and look at it for the next twenty days in your living room while your child opens a door a day.

If you have more than one child, don't feel that you have to choose one or make several calendars. Allow each child to open a door, sack, boot or parcel in rotation - teaching little ones to share in other people's excitement and pleasure when not necessarily receiving anything themselves is an invisible gift to them and a valuable lesson.

For an older member of the family - perhaps grandparents - and especially those who live further away or in a different country, how about printing out twenty-four photos of your family (making sure that they are not too big or else the whole thing will become enormous!) and paint your own picture in which to cut the twenty-four doors used to conceal and then reveal the photos. How about drawing or painting a tree as your main picture and positioning a photo at the end of each branch? (Most of us can attempt and produce something which resembles a tree!) It can be *your* family tree, and imagine the pleasure it will bring, not just in the run up to Christmas, but which can go on to be enjoyed all through the year.

If this is too complicated - and there is always the question of how you are going to transport/post it to its destination - why not place the photos in twenty-four numbered envelopes. Children might enjoy decorating each envelope for their grandparents or aunts, uncles and cousins.

'Whatever you decide to make, do or give, always try to encourage and involve others in its preparation. 'Whether you are working alone or with help, try to keep it as simple as possible and always remember to *enjoy* what you are doing and include some love.

Happy planning, plotting and making!

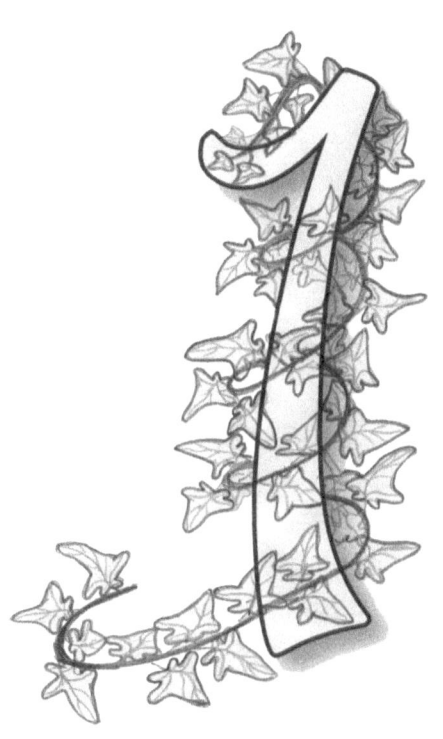

Door N° 1

Give everyone you see today a smile

It is such an incredibly simple and easy thing to do... isn't it? Smile. Just smile. But it can have a tremendous effect on those around you who see you smiling.

Think how you yourself feel when you see someone else smiling... it instantly tells you a great deal about what is happening and sets the whole scene for what will transpire... it lifts our spirits, calms and comforts us and puts us at our ease.

Conversely, how do you feel when you see someone frowning? It might be that they are only concentrating hard on something, but it immediately sounds warning bells... all is not well here... all is not right... and so we instantly begin to react by tensing our bodies, pushing away happy thoughts and literally depressing our own natural exuberance as we too turn our whole demeanour into a more negative state compatible with that of the other person.

There are so many people who might benefit from a cheery smile from you today. People in the street, on the bus, train or tube... folk in your workplace whom you do not know, have never spoken to. How might a smile from you lift their mood and brighten their lives, if only briefly? Think of all the people who might desperately need to see a friendly, smiling face. All the mothers and fathers who may have sick children lying at home. Or the people who are learning to rise to the ultimate challenge of physical or mental ill-health themselves. Think of the many among us who are mourning and grieving for the loss of a loved one. Also remember all the people struggling with harsh working hours and conditions and the millions among us who are fighting to combat debt.

Do you fall into any of those categories yourself? Don't feel you can raise a smile yourself? Doing so is all part of your gift to the world. Often it can be fun but no one said it would always be easy. That is no reason not to try though. Gandhi once said that we must be the change we wish to see in the world and what better way to start the ball rolling than by lifting the general mood around us with a smile? It also takes less physical effort. Our faces are full of tiny muscles which allow us to speak and eat and also eloquently express ourselves just by our facial expressions. It actually takes twenty-eight muscles to frown but only fourteen to smile. Less work. Less effort. Much better result!

Smiling is also good for us. We think of our faces as reflecting our intense emotional state but it can work both ways; we can influence and change our emotional state by altering our facial expression. When our brain receives the message that the muscles in our face are doing specific things - in this case smiling - then it will begin to physically react in certain beneficial ways.

Smiling promotes the production of the same 'feel good' hormones as when we exercise. Dopamine, endorphins and serotonin are all released into the blood stream, not only making us relax but also work to lower our heart rate and blood pressure. This in turn can help to reduce pain, regulate appetite and stimulate the immune system. In view of these effects it is perhaps not surprising to learn that one medical study has discovered that having the ability to truly smile throughout our life can increase life-expectancy by as much as seven years.

Other bonuses are that smiling helps to make us look younger, helps people to like us, is contagious and creates harmony around us, boosts activity and productivity and lowers anxiety. It is even good for our skin because it lifts the face, emphasizes cheek bones and lips and makes us look more attractive.

The whole idea of this alternative advent calendar is to give to others but in this first suggestion, as with many of the others, it is definitely a win-win situation for everyone. Think of all the marvellous benefits you are triggering in your own body as your smile broadens! But then think of the priceless gift you are giving to everyone else who smiles back at you today. Like a Tolkien or Harry Potter magician, what magic and miracles are you performing, just by being the reason that someone else has a smile on their face today?

World Smile Day - which was started by Harvey Ball, the business craftsman from Massachusetts who crafted the iconic yellow 'smiley face' back in 1963 - is now celebrated on the first Friday of November every year.

Let's have one of our own!

THINK ABOUT IT

Give the precious gift of a smile to everyone and everything today.

There is nothing so fundamentally positive, attractive, healing or life-changing as wearing a smile!

Door N° 2

Light a candle in the darkness

Light a candle. Literally. Preferably in a darkened room or space. Any candle will do; the plain white domestic version or a coloured dinner candle or a humble tea light. You may even choose to go out and buy a special Christmas candle. If you have nothing else to hand, even a half-used little birthday cake candle will suffice, although it will burn away to nothing in no time at all, so be aware. Ideally you want to give yourself time for contemplation... to stop and simply think for a while.

Sit with your candle for a few minutes and look deep into the heart of the flame. Look at the colours and shape. Feel the beauty and peace emanating from this single simple source of light and warmth. Notice how the flame resembles hands folded in prayer or gentle greeting. How does this make you feel?

At the approach of this, the darkest time of the year, all manner of lights are a traditional form of decoration. In particular candles encapsulate a deep relevance to the festive season for they have always been placed in windows to guide people home to safety and warmth and also to attract the spirits of natural green life of the outdoors to our homes where they can similarly find shelter. We bring these representational elements of life into our homes each Midwinter for safe keeping in the form of the evergreens with which we annually decorate our houses... holly, ivy, mistletoe, bay laurel, fir and pine.

How can we make ourselves into a similar beacon and more like the candle? How can we nourish and attract life, beauty and continuity? How can we keep this sacred light burning within ourselves as the outer world plunges ever further into physical darkness and moral and environmental anarchy and chaos?

There are other ways of metaphorically creating light. Some might feel that to perform an act of kindness, to cheer someone up, to show care and consideration - or just good manners - is to also symbolically light a candle in the darkness. Doing any of these things when you really don't feel like it makes your metaphorical candle shine even more brightly. Curiously, when you put yourself out on someone else's behalf, you usually feel much better. Making the extra effort always amply repays. Remember this when you are feeling decidedly uncooperative and grumpy with yourself!

For now, begin by lighting an actual candle first. Think about it. If nothing else, use this time to be kind to yourself. Give the gift of consideration to your own physical body. Listen to it and acknowledge how it is feeling and what these sensations are telling you.

Some of the activities suggested in the forthcoming days will provide a good start in helping you direct your thoughts and energies into becoming like a candle yourself and allowing your beautiful and perfect light to shine out.

You might wish to make yourself a simple advent wreath of evergreens and candles - it doesn't even have to be in the shape of a wreath - fill a pretty bowl with water and arrange a selection of evergreenery in it, along with the last of the autumn's colourful berries. Using a little melted wax from the bottom of the candles to stick four individual candles into low candle holders and place them around the outside of the bowl. Red candles are often used for this but, again, you can use whatever you wish or already have to hand.

There are a total of four Sundays in Advent, the last four Sundays before Christmas Day, one candle being lit on the first Sunday of Advent, two on the second Sunday and so on. Perhaps lighting your candles for a few minutes each day and just sitting quietly with them will bring much needed peace and clarity to the busy-ness of your day.

Model yourself on the candle - and let your light shine.

THINK ABOUT IT

Regularly allow yourself a little time to relax and just 'be'!

Someone who is calm and pleasant to be around is your gift to give for today-

And just like the candle, remember to let your light shine.

Door N° 3

Spend some quality time with someone

Spend a few minutes with someone and give them your whole attention.

Completely forget yourself.

Really listen to what they are saying.

No interrupting, no responding, no daydreaming... just truly listening with your whole self.

Look into the other person's eyes as they are speaking - tune out from the rest of the world around you - focus on them and them alone.

Be slow to speak yourself - perhaps be more inclined to communicate your care and empathy for them in other ways; smiling, holding their hand, putting an arm around their shoulders.

When your little conversation comes to an end, give that other person a really big, warm hug, and hold/leave your arms around them for several seconds - twenty seconds if possible as this stimulates healthful hormonal activity. Or, if you - or they - are more comfortable with holding hands or a light touch on the arm or shoulder, then do that instead. Just remember that many people never have any physical contact with another human being which can result in feelings of extreme isolation.

It doesn't matter who you are with. You might choose to give this gift of your deep attention and time to someone very close to you. We often inadvertently neglect those closest to us, just because they are so close to us. We feel that we can be with them... talk to them... any time we like so it gets put off again and again.

Or we might choose to bestow this lovely gift of sincere and gentle attention on a neighbour... someone we don't know very well... or someone we haven't seen or heard from in a while.

Remember that many of us are frequently beset by fears and worries. It doesn't matter that we usually get upset or frightened about something that hasn't actually yet happened - and probably never will. The threat of it in the current moment is all too real.

The old saying that a trouble shared is a troubled halved is very true. Somewhere in the telling it is often diminished and cut down to more manageable proportions. It helps us find a more realistic perspective. But folk won't be inclined to open up to someone who is constantly in a rush or never appears to be listening. We often have the wisdom within ourselves to solve our own problems. Spending time with someone who is caring and receptive helps us to find our courage.

Many people are lonely. Even those who appear to have lots of family and friends can be desperately lonely. The most effective place to experience loneliness is in a huge crowd where you are surrounded by people... but there is no one amongst them to whom you are important or matter. So, give the gift of showing someone that they matter to you. It might even be a total stranger.

It really does work best if you are actually with the person, sitting next to them in the same room, but it is possible to achieve a similar effect by talking over the phone - and I do mean talking, not texting. A lot of unspoken meaning can be conveyed by the voice, as can a great deal of genuine compassion and sympathy. It is also possible to convey attention by the depth of your silences, your considered replies and your willingness to remain on the phone rather than attempting to cut a conversation short and dash away as so many of us often end up doing. It takes time and dedication to hold a proper, in-depth conversation.

Or you might choose to give some of your time to someone you don't know at all - the elderly person sitting at the next table in the cafe or next seat on the bus - perhaps it might be the only opportunity they get to actually talk to someone that day... or that week... or, tragically, even month. Or perhaps a parent coping with one or more boisterous children. So often, parents, especially with young children, feel that everyone around them is judging their child's behaviour or their personal ability to be a 'good parent'. Help to set their minds at rest... and perhaps find that opening in which you can extend the great courtesy of truly listening to and hearing them.

Sometimes you don't have to say anything at all - it is enough to sit in a companionable silence. After all, just because we aren't actually speaking doesn't mean that we aren't communicating by being in someone's personal space and by the way we are sitting, the expression on our face... maybe just by silently holding that person's hand.

Be there for someone today.

THINK ABOUT IT

Forget yourself.
Think about someone else.

Give them your absolute and undivided attention... true quality time.

Door N° 4

Make someone a hot or cold drink

Well, that isn't too taxing, is it? But there is a little more to it than just the usual hurried slopping and scooping of ingredients into cups or mugs. On this occasion you need to concentrate on what you are really creating while you are preparing it. Put a bit of love, care and attention into what you are doing.

Who are you making it for? And why? Are they a family member? Are they exhausted because they have been working too hard? Or are they unwell? Are they elderly? Perhaps you need to borrow a little bit of yesterday's activity to go with this one? Don't just make them a drink; spend a few minutes with them while they drink it. If it is for a child or someone elderly, maybe you can put your arm around their shoulders, give them a hug - just hold them tenderly - while they are enjoying their drink? Lift their day.

Or perhaps you wish to buy a hot drink for someone who is homeless and out on the street? We all regularly walk past people in this predicament. Have you thought of asking them if they would like a hot drink? And if so, what would they prefer? Some people love tea and hate coffee, and vice versa. How do they prefer their tea, anaemically weak or terribly strong? How do they like it? Or they might really prefer a hot chocolate instead. Even if it is cold on the streets, they may be craving a bottle of pure orange juice or a pint of milk. These people have preferences just like anyone else. Extend them the courtesy to ask them. And if you can afford it, why not ask them if they would like a piece of cake or a sandwich, or a seasonal mince pie?

When you are giving it to them, don't just thrust it into their hands and rush off because you feel shy, embarrassed, self-conscious - you aren't doing this for you. Stop thinking about yourself and turn your full attention to the person who you are offering the drink to. Spend a couple of minutes talking to them - remember they are human beings, just like you, with feelings, hopes, dreams and fears. Again, it might help to remember yesterday's activity - be fully there with them. One minute of truly and fully being with a person is worth so much more than ten minutes shuffling from foot to foot while you feel awkward and tongue-tied and obviously cannot wait to get away.

Do you know that through your interactions with others you are actually demonstrating to the rest of the world what you think about yourself? That when you - apparently justifiably - become irritated, awkward and uncomfortable by someone or something, you are revealing your innermost feelings about yourself through your reactions? Or that when you turn a situation around and make people feel better or bring a smile to their face, you are really hanging out a huge sign about yourself for all the world to see and understand?

So, how are you doing so far? Are you enjoying yourself? Because it's all very well doing 'good' or 'nice' things for others, but if it makes you miserable, it really isn't going to benefit anyone in the end. Being stretched is fine... being pushed a little way out of your comfort zone is good... but being petrified with embarrassment and made miserable and awkward is not the goal!

The whole point of this Alternative Advent Calendar is to get us all thinking about others and not just focusing on what we want ourselves, but there must also be an element of personal enjoyment and satisfaction. Spread joy and fulfilment throughout your world - the whole world - and help to make it a happier more fun place to live in. Yes, service to others - and even a measure of self-sacrifice - is woven into the very meaning and fabric of the Christmas/Midwinter celebration in general and this advent calendar in particular, but not at the expense of all fun and pleasure.

Have a great day... and make someone else's day great too.

THINK ABOUT IT

Reach out to others.

Demonstrate that you have noticed them... and that you care.

Door N° 5

Play the part of St. Nicholas

In the Netherlands the 5th December is a very special day for it is the eve of Saint Nicholas' Day. Here (and also in some eastern European countries) children leave clogs or shoes out on Saint Nicholas' Eve to be filled with presents. They also believe that if they leave some hay and carrots in their shoes for '*Sinterklaas*' horse' they will be left some sweets. In the Netherlands much more is made of Saint Nicholas and his feast day than Christmas itself.

Children gather in the streets with their families while Saint Nicholas, accompanied by his companion *Zwarte Piet* (Black, Shock-haired or Wild Peter), travels on his cart or sleigh through the community. If they have been good children, they will receive their rewards from a generous and benign saint, but if they have been naughty, they run the risk of getting a beating from Wild Peter, or at the very least no present, or simply a lump of coal or handful of cinders.

Some believe that this tradition stemmed from the generosity of Nicholas, who was a Greek Christian bishop of Myra in Southern Turkey in the fourth century, and who anonymously gave money to poor girls who had no dowry.

It is often suggested that the archetypal figure of Father Christmas grew out of the generous saint's various activities and that the Dutch Reformed Church settlers took the beliefs and customs with them when they migrated to the Americas. This is probably not so. Rather it was the German immigrants in Pennsylvania who carried the tradition of *Pelznickel* which translates as 'furry Nickolas' who had a soot-blackened face, carried a bell and whip and was dressed from head to foot in fur with deep pockets filled to overflowing with nuts and cookies. On Christmas Eve *Pelznickel* would shyly flit from house to house, slipping down each chimney and depositing his gifts in the stockings left waiting for him. Here, surely, it is easy to see the forerunner characteristics of our own jovial but secretive Father Christmas or Santa!

It is from this dark, shaggy figure that Saint Nicholas' companion, Black or Wild Peter has developed, and he is altogether much older than Saint Nicholas. This tradition possibly has its origins rooted in the dim and distant past, long before Christianity came into being. Nor is Wild Peter the sole threat to children's happiness and harmony at this time of year for in past centuries, Saint Nicholas was once equally as fierce and frightening.

We do not tend to celebrate Saint Nicholas' Day in Britain, although it is based on ancient beliefs and practices which were once common to us all in the more northerly regions of the Northern Hemisphere.

As adults many of us go quietly about our every-day lives and no one seems to notice what we do, what we say, the efforts we make to look smart, work hard, be fair and helpful to others, and so on. So perhaps you can help redress the balance?

For today, you are going to take the part of Saint Nicholas! You are going to be the one to notice other people. How they look, what they are wearing, how they are behaving, perhaps something that they always do (like making you a cup of coffee) which you might normally appear to take for granted.

YOU will be their Saint Nicholas and acknowledge them, give them a little 'gift' in the form of a 'thank you', a compliment or some praise.

In other words, find something nice/complimentary/positive to say to everyone you meet today... and SAY it to them. Never mind that you feel shy or self-conscious or that they might think you have suddenly gone slightly mad - do it anyway. Remember, you aren't doing this for yourself, you are doing it to spread the light and love of the coming Midwinter/Christmas season.

And when you have plucked up the temerity, the courage to brighten someone's day by acknowledging and thanking them for who and what they truly are, how does it make you feel'?

Enjoy your new role for the day!

THINK ABOUT IT

A brief acknowledgement - a kind word - a simple 'thank you'.

It doesn't cost you anything.

But it will make a huge difference to the people you bestow them on.

Try following in ancient footsteps and keep one of the oldest traditions alive.

Door N° 6

Sing a Christmas carol

Don't sing? How about humming or whistling instead?

Don't like Christmas carols? Really? Not any of them? Come on. There must be one or two tunes amongst them that you like? You don't even have to subscribe to Christian belief - the music is lovely in its own right. Or if you really must, how about a modern Christmas song? Help us all get into the swing of things.

For those among you who do enjoy their carols, which ones do you like best? And why?

They are such an integral element to our Midwinter celebrations that I wonder if we tend to really listen to the lovely melodies or even hear the words any more? Have you really looked at some of the words of even our most famous carols? Try reading them as poems or prose - not as songs - some of the story-telling is lovely and in a few - like 'It Came Upon A Midnight Clear' - the words are deeply dramatic.

For me, some carols are so evocative of my beloved winter woodland - 'In the Deep Midwinter' and 'The Holly and the Ivy' being two of them. What child hasn't at some time or other sung 'Away in a Manger'? How many parents have proudly listened to their little offspring warbling 'Little Town of Bethlehem' or 'Silent Night'? Some people really get drawn into the rousing anthems:- 'Joy to the World' and 'Oh Come All Ye Faithful'. Perhaps this is one of the drawbacks to such emotive singing? We all have a plethora of memories and emotions attached to each carol, which is why it might be difficult for some of us to sing - or even hear - certain tunes and songs.

Like various scents, sounds and music resonate and encompass such depth and variety of emotion.

The word carol comes from the French word *carole* which means to process in a circle dance with singing. Originally, they weren't just performed at Christmas but throughout the year in honour of every season. Surprisingly they were not considered quite religiously respectful and for many years kept firmly outside the church. We have people like Edward White Benson to thank for changing the whole attitude towards these popular colloquial songs. In 1880 he was bishop of Truro and wished to encourage his congregation to leave the festivities in the pubs on Christmas Eve and attend a church service instead. The bishop hit upon the idea of a Christmas carol service - the nine lessons and carols which we all now recognise as an integral and traditional part of Christian Christmas celebration.

Perhaps appealing to the masses goes back much further though, to thirteenth century Europe, when all church services and hymns were conducted and sung in Latin. In France and Germany, and particularly Italy under the influence of Saint Francis of Assisi, a strong tradition of popular Christian songs in regional native languages developed.

John Awdlay, a Shropshire chaplain in 1426, lists twenty-five carols of 'Cristemas', probably sung by wassailers at communal secular celebrations like harvest thanksgiving and new year. Some of our oldest carols are the 'Coventry Carol' and 'The First Nowell' which have their origins in the Fourteenth Century and 'Deck the Halls' and 'Adeste Fidelis' which can be traced back to the Sixteenth Century. But it was in the Eighteenth and Nineteenth Centuries that folklorists began to collect popular Christmas folk songs and smarten them up - and were also inspired to write new ones too.

Words and music were frequently written by different people, often years apart. We have to thank people like William Sandys and David Gilbert, and later Ralph Vaughan Williams and Percy Dearmer for finding and saving much of our best loved folk music, along with some of our most popular Christmas carols.

When and where you sing your carol is entirely up to you. Perhaps while you are on your own in the bath or shower? or in the kitchen preparing a meal? or quietly to yourself while you are walking down the street? Or if you need a bit of moral support, find carol singing on YouTube and sing along with your computer. If you really feel like going public with this suggestion, you could always find somewhere doing Christmas karaoke.

Whatever your feelings about Christmas carols, just for today, give it a go - you might surprise yourself, and cheer us all into the bargain... blessings, and good luck!

THINK ABOUT IT

Forget yourself - blast out a rousing tune - sing, whistle or just hum... words don't matter - simply enter into the season in wholehearted, enthusiastic celebration!

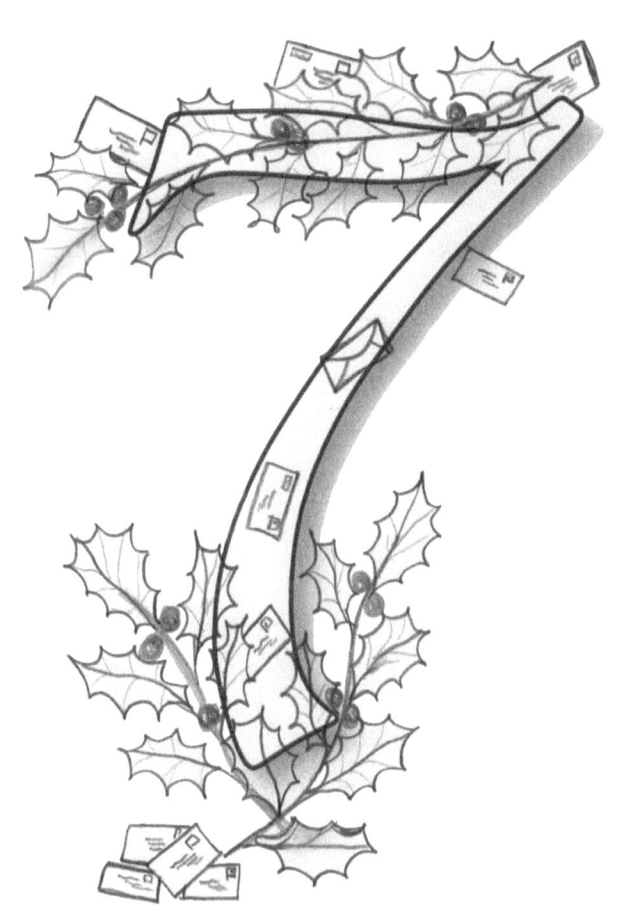

Door N° 7

Write a seasonal card to a neighbour

How many of your neighbours do you know? I mean really know well enough that you could quite happily stop and have a chat to them? These days it seems that most of us barely recognise those living close to us. Some of us have absolutely no idea at all... and sadly couldn't care less.

Of course, we all have our own busy and independent lives to lead. But these other people who live within a mere few yards of you share the very air you breath, the views you see every day, the road you walk or drive down. If there is a problem with security or the environment, you will all likely be affected by it. In many ways you are all in the same proverbial boat.

Also, remember that we are all connected to each other on many levels. Modern science has proved that all twenty-first century humanity is 99.9% genetically the same. This has even more relevance for people who still live in the same area that their ancestors inhabited over many generations. Very likely people who also hail from the same geographical area have married into your family and intermixed many times over the centuries. They are truly your brothers and sisters at one remove. People from other parts of the globe are just a little more distant, so you might like to look on them as your cousins instead. But we are ALL close.

We are also close in the fact that we all share so many life experiences. We all of us know what it is like to fall in love, to grieve for a lost one, to have dreams, to laugh and cry, to feel hungry or afraid, to be happy and excited. Look beyond the strange face, the different coloured skin, the foods, clothes and ways of celebrating that seem odd and sometimes threatening to us. Look beyond these unimportant details. This person living next door to you sleeps and breathes and worries and hopes... just like you do.

It costs nothing to be pleasant and put on a friendly face... say a few cheery words... it oils the wheels of our most personal society. It enables people to then be able to approach one another with tolerance and understanding, to be heard, and hopefully, also to be willing to listen.

So if there is someone living on your street, down your road, in your block and you have never yet spoken to them, why not write them a seasonal card? (If you aren't sure what their spiritual/religious beliefs are, make sure that it doesn't display specific and possibly offensive illustrations or language) and then go and knock on their door, introduce yourself and tell them that you are using this as an opportunity to get to know them. Smile. Don't be put off if they respond with bewilderment or suspicion. Leave it at that... and then try again on some other occasion. They might think you a busy-body or a nuisance, but at least they will know that you exist!

Conversely, they might be really glad to make proper contact with someone living close by. We don't have to be elderly or unwell to feel isolated and vulnerable. Just understanding who lives around us can be amazingly comforting and helps to make a micro-community within the wider one. And neighbours can do so many practical and positive things for each other: take delivery of post or parcels, hold a spare key in case you lock yourself out, feed your cat, get your washing in if it rains, pick up a couple of items for you along with their own grocery shop, keep an eye on your property when you aren't there...

There are so many benefits to being a 'good neighbour' - so this Christmas give your local community the gift of being one today.

THINK ABOUT IT

Reach out to someone and make that connection - start enriching your personal community today.

Door N° 8

Give yourself the gift of freedom

Today you are going to give something to your own brain and body - you are going to give them a rest. Obviously, we can't all suddenly take a holiday from work and commitments but you can take a holiday from yourself. You can stop pouring all that stress and pressure on yourself. You can silence those grating voices within you which unendingly criticise and make you feel guilty and small for all your supposed short-comings and failures. You can stop worrying about all that you still have to achieve and accomplish. You can give yourself a break from all your fears that will, in all likelihood, never actually materialise. You can even let go of your dreams and aspirations for a few hours... sometimes they too can be relentless taskmasters.

If you are brave enough you can also switch off your phone and step away from the computer. Go on, be adventurous - start a new fashion... the 'unconnected trend'! Give yourself some peace and space to breath, to think... if you dare?

Wherever you are, stop what you are doing for a couple of minutes and take a look around you. Really look around you. It doesn't matter if you are just pottering along doing repetitive, mundane chores.

What do you see?

How do you feel about where you currently are? Whether it is your home or where you work, is it a nice place? Does it make you feel whole, happy, fulfilled, festive and positive? Or does it leave you feeling down, depleted, overwhelmed, sad or negative?

What can you do to magnify the positive aspects of your surroundings and what can you do to decrease or eliminate the negative ones? Jot your ideas down on a piece of paper, resolving to make those changes when you are ready - but not today.

Today, you are going to give yourself permission to be empowered. You have silenced your self-doubt and criticism - at least temporarily. You have put all your commitments to one side. You have taken decisions to change your surroundings for the better. Now you are going to walk away from it all. Yes, you can. Even if it is just for half an hour. They say that a change is as good as a rest and you will be all the fresher and more able to complete your tasks afterwards.

Wrap up warmly. Step outside into the winter air. Look out for the natural world - whether you live in a rural area or the middle of a busy town or city nature is always all around us; there are always trees, weeds, front gardens, birds, parks and flower beds to be found. And what about the weather? That is everywhere, all the time. What is it doing today? We tend to forget that the weather - which we British love to comment on and complain about - is just another facet of the natural world.

What do you see? Bare branches? Dead stalks? What else? Look for tiny green buds on tree branches and bushes. Keep an eye out for small tips of green spears where snowdrop and daffodil shoots have already pushed through the earth. Spring really is just around the corner! What can you see of the festive season? Lights in shops? Decorations in streets?

House windows full of Christmas trees or other colourful decorations. Red berries on holly bushes? Winter jasmine?

Just walk around and take it all in. This is your day... this is your present... your time... here and now. Make the very most of it and enjoy it to the full. We miss so much, especially in the run up to the Midwinter/Christmas celebrations. What do you like or appreciate about your outdoor surroundings? What would you like to change? How might you go about doing that? When you return indoors, jot down your thoughts next to the ones you commented on about your indoor surroundings. Put them at the back of your diary and when it comes time to celebrate the new year, take them out and make them a part of your New Year resolutions.

This is your world, and this is you in it. Make the most of it!

THINK ABOUT IT

This is your world and your life within it.

Take a good long hard look at it and make it into what you really want.

Door N° 9

Give Christmas Hugs to Everyone

This is actually one of the nicest and most beneficial things that you can do for another person.

I am not talking about the brief courtesy action of dipping one's head forward to give or receive a brief 'air kiss' on either side of your head. Do not mistake a cuddle for a hug either. Cuddles mean something slightly different... nestling together, being close and snug for a prolonged amount of time. I am referring to taking someone in your arms and clasping them to you warmly and wholeheartedly for a number of seconds.

To be gently and tenderly held by another, heart to heart, is both emotionally relaxing and very supportive. But more than that, a hug lasting twenty seconds or more stimulates the vagus nerve and the parasympathetic nervous system which in turn acts as a tonic for our circulatory system, lowers blood pressure, reduces the physical effects of stress and a dozen other wonderful things.

For a start, hugging someone helps to build a sense of trust and safety and helps to open honest communication. Admittedly, one has to have even a tiny measure of these before one can open up to giving or receiving a hug in the first place but build on even the tiniest fragment that is there... in yourself and others.

Hugging helps to teach us how to give and receive and how to be present in the moment. It can also encourage us to flow with the energy of life, get you out of circular thinking patterns and connect you with your heart, your feelings and your breath. The energy exchange between two people hugging each other encourages empathy and understanding... the whole is more than the sum of its parts.

Research findings suggest that associations of self-worth and tactile sensations from our early years are still embedded in our nervous systems as adults. The memory of hugs we received earlier in our young lives remain at a cellular level and hugs in adulthood remind us of that at a somatic level. Therefore, hugs can also connect us to our ability to self-love.

Research has also shown that hugging someone is extremely effective at healing sickness, disease, loneliness, depression, anxiety and stress. It helps to relax your muscles and in so doing can ease physical tension which in turn can help to remove pain and sooth aches by allowing increased blood circulation into soft tissue.

Hugging has also been shown to help to balance the nervous system. The galvanic skin response of someone giving and receiving a hug shows a change in skin conductance. The effect in skin moisture and electricity on the surface of the skin suggests a more balanced state in the parasympathetic nervous system.

Just as importantly, hugging stimulates the body's production of oxytocin, more commonly known as the 'love hormone' which benefits mental health conditions such as depression and anxiety. This is because oxytocin is a neurotransmitter which acts on the brain's emotional centre promoting feelings of trust, contentment, intimacy and bonding. Oxytocin also helps to decrease levels of the stress hormone, cortisol, which in turn will help the heart to stay healthier.

Hugging also aids the production of serotonin - another neurotransmitter - and dopamine which is also responsible for regulating our emotional response and reward circuit in the brain. Lack of both these hormones is usually implicated in people who suffer from mood disorders, depression and insomnia.

Perhaps it is then not so surprising to learn that hugging can also strengthen the immune system. Gentle physical pressure on the sternum (breastbone) and solar plexus (area just below your ribcage) creates an emotional charge which stimulates the thymus gland which, in turn, regulates and balances the body's production of white blood cells keeping us healthy and disease free. Research has concluded that healthy adults who receive regular hugs are less likely to get a head cold and even those who do will suffer less severe symptoms.

Finally, it has been estimated that for a healthy life we need a certain number of hugs each day - four for survival, eight for good maintenance and twelve for growth. This is a different kind of 'five a day' but apparently equally as important!

So, go on, help to make the world an infinitely better place - give someone an early Christmas present today - something of real benefit to them.... give them a hug!

THINK ABOUT IT

Hugging someone is so simple

yet might be the most important thing that you ever do for that person.

Door N° 10

Feed the birds

This morning I awoke to frost silvering the grass, a clear cold sky and the stark outline of the Nantlle Ridge mountains, coal black against the paling dawn. Beautiful! What one thinks of as typical winter weather, and so it is, but winter weather isn't always easy or pleasant for the wildlife trying to exist outside in it.

Take the bird population for instance. Many of our best-loved species are under threat... from loss of habitat, pesticides, the change in weather patterns and shortage of food. Spare them a thought.... and more than a thought... do something to help them.

If you are going out shopping today, you might like to buy an extra gift... a gift for the birds outside your home. Wherever you live, whether it is in the middle of a city or out in suburbia, by the sea or in the countryside, there will be birds living around or not very far from you... large or small... they all need to eat. Some types of bird are required to consume their own weight in food each day just to survive.

So why not buy a bag of mixed bird seed (which will appeal to more than one type of feathered friend), or some fat balls, or nuts? (You may prefer to make your own fat balls, which is fine in winter but may melt too quickly in summer.) I have a family of blackbirds who are addicted to white bread and (unfortunately) my holly berries!

Be aware that, similar to us, birds need fresh food in clean containers. Always remove any stale food not eaten after an appropriate length of time and once a week take apart and thoroughly wash/scrub all feeders and dishes getting into all the nooks and crannies with a dilute disinfectant. Rinse thoroughly so that all harmful chemicals are also removed after cleaning. Many of our best-loved birds are suffering and dying from salmonella due to eating stale food from dirty containers.

Also remember that not all food which is good for us is similarly good for our little feathered friends. Some kitchen scraps such as pastry, meat and tinned pet food, cooked potato, cheese, rice, dried fruits and oats are fine as is a reasonable amount of bread. Milk, desiccated coconut, polyunsaturated margarines and vegetable oils and soft fats are definitely bad or dangerous for wild birds.

Popping some food out for the birds can become quite a complex business considering that different birds require different types of food and eat best in different locations - on the ground, in trees, from feeders, and so on. Good quality seed mixes and fat balls sold specially for wild garden birds will provide a decent staple. The R.S.P.B. provide lots of information, both on their website and in simple, easy to read and follow leaflets. If you really care about your local wildlife, just spend a few minutes looking up what is best for them.

Don't forget that birds also need a source of fresh, clean water, both to drink and to bath in. When the weather is cold and dry or frosty and frozen they can suffer great hardship through dehydration so place one or two flat bowls or plates of water out for them and change every day. If the weather is freezing, refresh the water in them twice a day. Also remember that predatory cats may be around so try to place your water and edible offerings in a safe spot; somewhere the birds will be able to easily see the approach of a predatory animal and fly away safely in good time.

Be aware that your local birds will need food and water on a regular basis. In severe weather, feed twice daily, in the morning and again in the early afternoon. But if you do establish a feeding routine, try not to change it as the birds will come to expect food at certain times and can suffer great stress when it isn't forthcoming.

Thinking of the approaching Winter Solstice , you might wish to get up a Midwinter feast for your wild birds, to help mark the occasion but it is more important to provide a moderate amount of food constantly through the leanest months than have a glut and dearth.

Think about it - see what you can do - even if it is only a very little, give it to the natural world with love and gratitude... and watch the marvellous display that your gift will attract!

Enjoy!

THINK ABOUT IT

We humans have taken - stolen - so much from the

natural world.

It is time to take responsibility.

Give something back!

Door N° 11

Leave a message of loving kindness in a public place

A lot of people will be feeling pre-Christmas stress and it will really start to intensify now. For some it will be not having enough time or energy to do all that they would like to make Christmas for their loved ones. For others it will be not having a clue how they are going to divide their time over the holiday period so that all their family and in-laws see enough of them. Many will be agonising over the cost of the festive period. Whilst for some, it will be facing the Midwinter celebrations alone, or at least without their beloved. And so it goes...

If you are going out to the shops today, take a look around you. You simply cannot tell just by looking at people's faces what is going on beneath the surface. So, before you go, tear a piece of paper from a notebook, write a kind message on it, fold it a couple of times so it is small - but not too small - and take it with you. When you find somewhere you think someone will find your message, leave it there... how about propped by the condiments in a cafe, or tucked between the packets of biscuits in the supermarket, or down the back of a seat on the bus? Somewhere it won't be ignored but won't attract too much attention. I'm sure that you can spot lots of good places.

Someone doesn't necessarily have to be in crisis to benefit from a kindly word. We all have days when we could really benefit from a friendly or thoughtful word. On the other hand, there are so many people who are living with intolerable difficulties and facing huge challenges. Many of what we think of as 'normal' lives are actually fraught with difficulty and heartbreak.

Don't try to think too hard about what you might write either. Keep it light and unambiguous. What do you wish for your reader? A happy day? Sunshine and happiness in their life? Appreciation, recognition and support? Tell them so. Include the fact that although you have never met, you are thinking about them today and they matter to you. Wish them well in loving friendship. It is a real gift for people not to feel so isolated and alone.

If you easily get embarrassed offering such a message, doing it anonymously in this way spares your own blushes and frazzled nerves. It also allows the person who finds it to quietly read it and take it in... and re-read it as many times as they wish. The spoken word is wonderfully powerful but we often do not remember what has been said, especially if it is unexpected. It is lovely to be able to return to something and relive it as much as we like.

Your simple words might make ALL the difference to someone today... might just tip the balance between them coping, coming through, making a success, or giving up and possibly losing everything. In the past there have been many accounts of people who have decided to commit suicide, or leave their families or walk away from a job they normally love, until a chance encounter with someone who was kind to them - just in the normal, everyday way of things - provided them with a different perspective; a little comfort in their fear, a little light in their darkness... some hope.

We don't have to be on the very edge of such a terrible precipice either. Who doesn't appreciate a kind word? a bit of encouragement or appreciation? We all tend to relax, bloom and expand with appreciation and encouragement.

So go valiantly forth. No one will know what you are doing so you don't have to feel nervous about being thought odd or silly. Put your heart into your message - if you feel inspired to do so, write several. With love.

Good luck!

THINK ABOUT IT

There is the old saying about 'casting your bread upon the water'.

You never know where it will end up, who it might feed...

or when it might find its way back to you in your time of need.

Door N° 12

Phone or message a friend who you haven't spoken to in a while

You know the ones! The dear friend you are constantly making notes for in your head... "Oooh, she'd love to hear that..." "Ooooh, he'd be so amused to know...." Often the people we feel closest to are the ones who get ignored because we feel close enough to leave them till last while we attend to all the other pressing 'have to's'.

And then there is the opposite end of the scale - all the people who you genuinely enjoy receiving a Christmas card or message from but suddenly remember that you haven't contacted for months - or sometimes years.

Any day of the year is a good time to get in touch with people you care about but don't have the opportunity to see or speak to very often. Midwinter or Christmas celebration gives us a reminder, an excuse to do so. At least once a year we are provided with a reason to make that effort.

Make a phone call to someone you haven't spoken to for a while and surprise them. Don't make a nuisance of yourself. Ask them if they have the time now for a bit of a chat or should you phone back another time?

Or fire off a jolly and enthusiastic email. Find a photo to accompany it. Keep it brief but include the invitation for that person to respond knowing that it will be warmly received and appreciated. Surprise someone and lift their day out of the hum-drum - provide them with something to smile about and think about.

At this time of year, you might wish to consider catching up with lots of people in one fell swoop by composing a 'round robin' letter to accompany your seasonal card. Don't groan! It isn't just what you do, it is the manner in which you do it that can make all the difference. Whatever you write, make it relevant and authentic. At least once in the twelve-month cycle it is wonderful to be able to pour out all your news... and try not to hold back. If you have had a good year, rejoice in sharing your good fortune with your dear ones. If you have had a terrible time, gently let everyone know that too, but also try to balance negative news with positive perspectives for the future. Whilst being realistically truthful you also need to avoid being darkly depressing. Bear in mind that some people might have had a much worse year than you so try to deliver less savoury news gently. Make your messages as genuine as possible, but also don't be afraid to include detail, humour and reality.

Perhaps you are lucky to have the time and opportunity to sit and write your letters individually. For many of us, the constraints upon our time and energy make this unlikely or impossible. But at least while you are writing your letter, bring to mind as many of the people to whom you are addressing it as possible. There is also always the option of personalising your letters with some individual hand-written comments after it is printed out.

It is of the utmost importance to really mean what you think, write and say. Words have a potency that we often choose to ignore or give credit for. They have a life of their own - an energetic resonance as real as any physical action, so make sure that each thought comes straight from your heart for, be under no illusion, it will find its mark.

Or perhaps you might consider recording a seasonal message to send out on Facebook or other social media? You might like to wear something special - although it really isn't necessary, it is your face that everyone will be focusing on. Watch your background - it can be terribly distracting to see someone talking to you with a houseplant or lampshade apparently sprouting out of the top of their head. If you tend to dry up or lose your words; if you are nervous or are afraid that you won't say what you actually want, write your message down and slowly read it, remembering to hold your paper up so that even as you read your face is still visible to the camera, and every so often, pause and look directly at it. Relax... and don't forget to smile!

So pick up your phone... now, this minute... make that call. Pick up a pen and set it to paper. Get out whatever device you can record with. Start thinking what you would like to say. Connect with those who really mean something to you and let them know just how much you care... Today.

THINK ABOUT IT

This time of year, above all others, is the time to reach out.

Because of the season, people will be more likely to be receptive to you.

A new year is coming, so take this opportunity to make the world - your world - a more connected, friendly and caring place.

Door N° 13

Give thankfulness & Gratitude

Beginning to feel the pressure now? Things still to do mounting up and time growing short? Getting tired and inclined to be tetchy? Then just stop for a minute. Take time to consider just how lucky you are. Yes, I said lucky. Because no matter how much work you have to do, how much preparation for the Winter Holiday, how many sticky situations with recalcitrant relatives you may be facing or how great the financial short-fall in your bank balance, there is still a great deal going for your life... here... now... this minute.

Think about it. What have you to feel grateful for? Look around you. No matter how you feel, you probably have a certain degree of health and ability to achieve something good this Midwinter. Do you have family or good friends? (And if you don't have any relatives to share it with, then at least you don't have to worry about awkward family members or someone causing a row.) You have warm clothes on your back, a roof over your head, something to eat today... the list goes on and can become far more refined. You are free to think, say, read what you like... free to go outside and breath the air without risk of bodily harm...

A word of warning, though. At this time of year especially the commercial world plays heavily upon our emotions and our feelings of self-worth. The inference is that to be happy and successful we must own certain items without which our lives are incomplete. Advertisers seek to instil a belief in the unfairness of life, a sense of entitlement that we are just as deserving as the next man or woman who has already purchased so many wonderful

- but usually superfluous - items. This can lead to us feeling a whole cocktail of unpleasant emotions; dissatisfaction, irritability, restlessness, grumbling and depression - even anger, resentment and rage with other people who are supposedly luckier than ourselves. Recognise this advertising entrapment of raising false expectations and feelings of lack for what it truly is - nonsense! Think about it carefully. Separate need from want.

I really love the whole concept of the American Day of Thanksgiving. A time to all come together. To set differences aside within the immediate family, to turn away from all the usual distractions of our lives and simply focus on our loved ones... and to assess our many blessings and give thanks for them. What is not to like? I feel that we should all celebrate 'thanksgiving'. The Americans celebrate their Thanksgiving Day at the end of November, but you might like to instigate your own unofficial day of thankfulness - bring the people you love together and revel in their company... their very being... and give thanks for it.

I have a dear friend who used to live next door to an elderly gentleman. After his wife died, despite grieving for her deeply, he continued to remain cheerful and always used to say "Well, I'm just going in now to count my blessings!"

We all have a great deal to be thankful for. Especially in these more uncertain times of political upheaval, global warming and civil unrest where stress, depression and sickness is rife and our youth are far less lucky - or happy - with their diminishing prospects. Look around you today and count your blessings... we all have far more than we think.

A good - and very positive - way of relaxing into refreshing sleep at the end of the day is to focus on all the things you are thankful for in the day you have just had. Or if there are too many - and I am not joking - simply pick out the very best and place all your attention on a single event or item that you are truly thankful for and mentally lose yourself in it as you drift off to sleep. Be strict with yourself. Under no circumstances allow other negative thoughts, worries or concerns to creep in. They will still be around whenever you choose to take them out and examine them... or maybe not. For whatever you think and feel changes the vibration and rhythms of your body and ultimately attracts more of the same to itself. You might wake up and find that some of your most threatening fears have simply melted away. Try it and see.

First and foremost is the prime importance of the fact that whatever else we do or do not have, we have today... this day. Without getting too maudlin, we all know that the human condition is uncertain - we can never be sure what is just around the corner. So, we might not be able to count on anything else, but we surely have what is around us this minute... we can surely own these next few seconds or hours. This is truly our time. We have this, now.

So here is something to definitely give thanks for. Grab this acknowledgement of life - your life - and fully live, breath and feel it. Are we joyful in the realisation of our precious seconds? If so, spread that joy. And give thanks.

THINK ABOUT IT

Be thankful; for the little things as well as the large

Count your blessings - not of abundance - but of having enough.

Door N° 14

Speak kindly to something in the natural world

It is good to remember the natural world. If you live in a busy town or city, you don't have to make a special journey out into the countryside to connect with it. It is all around you, wherever you are and whatever you are doing.

Look outside your window. 'What can you see'? Even if you are surrounded by concrete buildings and asphalt roads and pavements, it is usually still possible to spot a few blades of grass or weeds - even in winter. There are always birds too, even in the most built up and polluted areas.

Look up. 'What can you see now'? The sky is a part of the natural world, although we tend to ignore it, just because it is there with us wherever we go. 'You are now looking at our precious atmosphere - which we now all know we are wilfully damaging every day - but this fragile coating around our planet is what keeps us safe here and allows us to live on the surface of this Earth.

'What is the weather doing'? 'Raining... windy... frosty... dull, grey and damp... sunny with blue skies'? The weather is part of the natural world too and is also with us and around us wherever we are.

How often do we even notice all these aspects of our everyday life, let alone show any appreciation of them'? 'We habitually criticise the weather; if it is dry we fear drought, if it is wet we fear floods, if it is sunny it is too hot for us, if it is frosty or snowy it is too cold or an inconvenience and if it is overcast, grey and nondescript, we complain that we are depressed. How about being thankful for the fresh air we breath, the sufficient water that flows through our taps, the daylight which gives us life, the darkness of night-time which allows us to rest?

The trees planted along our streets and in our parks help to cleanse our air, as does every plant and shrub, (and if our air is polluted, who's responsibility is that?). The weeds growing in the cracks between the paving stones and tarmac are living plants - there is really no such thing as a 'weed'. There is an old saying that a weed is only a plant growing in the wrong place. Many of the plants which we regularly wage war on and eradicate from our domestic parks and gardens contain precious healing or nutritional components. Dandelions are an diuretic and make an excellent white wine; daisies for bruising, nettles contain iron and vitamin C and help to purify the blood; Japanese knotweed can be eaten as a vegetable and is, potentially, a valuable cancer treatment.

This is the day to notice and really understand that we share this planet with everything else and that we have our place amongst the natural world, not to the exclusion and detriment of everything else - that particular brand of irresponsibility and arrogance leads to annihilation for all of us. This is the day to literally open your eyes, minds and hearts to the living world that is around us... and voice our appreciation and gratitude.

If for some reason you can't get outside, even if you don't come across an animal in the fur, a bird in the feather, or a plant in the root today, think kind thoughts of loving appreciation about some particular and specific aspect of the natural world that is close to you. Speak them out loud. Our thoughts and spoken words transmute into energetic intention becoming tangible and do reach their target. Bless the rain. Welcome the daylight

- short and frequently dull and dark as it is at this time of year. Even better if you do see something in the natural world to pass your good wishes on to - even a little sparrow up in your guttering, a late and weary bumble bee, a spider or drowsy fly - they all have their place within the grand scheme of things and it is deserving of our loving attention. Anything and everything.

So, you feel silly talking to a blackbird or a thundercloud. When weighed against the positive good it can achieve, does it matter? Forget yourself and focus on the bigger picture here.

Say "Thank you - you are beautiful" - and mean it.

THINK ABOUT IT

Reach out and connect to the wonder of the natural world all around you.

We humans tend to isolate ourselves from all other life, unless it is sanitised and controlled out of all recognition.

Much of our ill health stems from our disconnection from nature.

Blessings to all.

Door N° 15

Give the gift of a good temper

We all do it. Accidentally drop something... stub our toe... forget something... and then we make snide comments to our self, usually referring to our self but also about others. In doing so, our mood changes. The peace or upbeat feeling of the day is shattered, the atmosphere becomes charged with something more unpleasant, and after that it is all too easy to become irritated and continue to make increasingly impatient and wounding little comments - aloud or inside one's head - until someone else enters the room and it can ignite into a full-blown row.

So, nip it in the bud. Listen to yourself. Diffuse a potential situation before it can develop. Next time you catch yourself telling yourself off, stop and grin at yourself. We are just human. Fallible. We all make mistakes... we all do daft things... it's part of living. But we can turn it all around... smile or laugh and shrug it off. Have you noticed how impossible it is to go on feeling cross if your facial features are smiling? Try it now. Something communicates from the physical to the emotional and can change our mood. Stop the rot in its tracks and generate a lighter feeling to your day.

If you tend to get annoyed or cross and angry quite easily, there are several simple and helpful things that you can do to try to help yourself feel better. Deep, slow breathing works well. Taking a brisk walk is also very effective - it removes you from the troubling situation while your body releases endorphins as you walk and when you are ready to deal with the situation you can walk back with a clearer head.

Find somewhere to be alone each day - somewhere you can relax. Play upbeat or relaxing music. Doing a few good stretches each morning when you first get out of bed can be helpful too. Using calming essential oils is a great way of combating stress and keeping you and your responses on a more even keel. Good quality lavender, rose and jasmine are just three amongst many which have a wonderful scent and are relaxing and healing, but there are literally hundreds for you to choose from. Use them in a burner or diffuser at home and carry a little glass bottle or jar containing a few drops for you to sniff regularly during the day.

Perhaps you might need to work out why you feel and react as you do? If certain things, places, people or situations aggravate you, try to avoid them or cut them out of your life completely. Try to identify a solution. Talk to someone you trust who might help you to get a different perspective on a situation.

Remember that if you lose your temper, you are no longer in control - the person or situation who has caused you to snap is. Do you really want something like that or someone like them to be controlling you?

If your short fuse has been generated by over-work - perhaps trying to do too much in preparation for giving everyone a 'good Christmas'- don't you think that your nearest and dearest might prefer to have a less fraught December even if it means a less spectacular Winter celebration? No one really likes a bad-tempered martyr!

If you are really having a bad day and cannot even muster a smile - and we all occasionally have days like this, admit it! - it sounds like something in your life is way out of balance and my heart goes out to you. So instead, take this day to be especially kind to yourself.

For the rest of us, the Advent challenge for today is to demonstrate a good temper. It is one of the best gifts that we can give to those around us, especially at this time of year when everyone is getting over excited, over tired and over stressed.

Smile when you feel grumpy. Say something kind when you feel irritated. Give someone a hug when you feel cross. Watch how differently everyone around you responds and how much better, lighter, positive your day becomes, and sense how differently you yourself feel... how all your rough edges simply melt away.

Smiles and hugs to you all!

THINK ABOUT IT

One of the greatest self-disciplines we can demonstrate is restraint.

If your day isn't as easy as you would wish, is it going to make you feel better by spoiling someone else's?

By refraining from upsetting someone else - more, by attempting to smooth things over - at least you won't have contributed to everyone's problems but you will likely have made everyone's day a whole lot better.

Door N° 16

Give a Christmas Stocking

As children, many of us - if we were lucky - have known the excitement of finding a bulging, knobbly stocking at the bottom of our bed on Christmas morning. The joy of lying in the dark, tentatively prodding, poking and investigating all the tantalisingly anonymous shapes and anticipating just what they might be could almost be more satisfying than unpacking it all!

Why not bring a measure of that same excitement and - in this case - unlooked-for pleasure and anticipation into the life of an adult this year? Perhaps an elderly relative or neighbour... or as an alternative Christmas gift for a work colleague or friend... or the harassed lass working flat out on the checkout at your local shop or supermarket... or the homeless person sitting in the street?

If you wish to avoid possible embarrassment you may wish to contrive to give your stocking anonymously. This can then become part of the gift - the mystery of trying to guess who might have done such a thing? This is also a kindness which can be extended at any time - not just Christmas - when someone is perhaps feeling sad or in need. Leave a little gift or a home made cake or a bag of fruit on someone's doorstep. They may guess who their benefactor is - it is up to you whether you own up to it or not!

Yes, it does take just a little time and thought but no, it doesn't have to involve much financial outlay - in fact it is better if doesn't because your actual gift is surprise, anticipation and a return to uncomplicated childhood rather than one of adult expense and glitz.

Start off by buying a pair of socks - ordinary socks or slipper socks - one of which will be used to hold everything else and the other one which you can roll up and stuff into the toe of your 'Christmas stocking' so that the pair may be worn normally after Christmas.

Of course, the rest of the contents may be as varied as you could possibly wish, but try and stick to useful and inexpensive with a dash of indulgence, so you might include things like a pen and notebook, a comb, nice soap, a bar of chocolate or a little bag of sweets... just simple, useful, everyday sort of items. Wrap each individual item and of course, don't forget to add the traditional prerequisites of an apple, clementine or orange and a few chocolate (or real) coins into the foot of the stocking along with its rolled-up mate.

If you know the person you wish to give a Christmas stocking to well, you might wish to develop a theme for the contents. Perhaps they are a cat or dog lover in which case you might want to find little gifts which reflect this - socks with cats or dogs on them, notebooks or shopping bags with a picture of their favourite animal on the front; pens, erasers, earrings or other jewellery related designs - use your ingenuity and have fun seeing what you can come up with. You can do something similar for someone who loves gardening or music or a particular sport. The possibilities are endless.

This form of presentation, (and consequent constriction on size), can be adapted to form a very special gift for someone close to you - perhaps the significant 'other' in your life.

But for now, just stick to cheap and cheerful... and that all-important element of surprise at being given what is, ostensibly, a child's gift, but with an adult interpretation. Having said that, planning a Christmas stocking for some unsuspecting grown-up can provide just as much pleasure for the giver as the recipient.

We often hear that we should learn to love ourselves. I would suggest that you forget yourself and think about others for a change. Bring out your sympathy and empathise - you will learn a whole lot about yourself in the process. You will also learn that you are not such a bad/silly/unloved person after all and you will begin to see - and accept - yourself in the light of your kindness to others. Yes, you might begin to see your faults more clearly too, but you will begin to recognise them for what they really are - minor details which can be modified, changed, or eliminated - merely the frail human trappings of the otherwise beautiful person which is really you.

It is said that to understand is to forgive. Perhaps as you begin to look at yourself and acknowledge your weak points you can also start to understand yourself a little better and not be so hard on yourself. I will repeat, just for now, forget yourself. Do this little thing for someone else. Bringing pleasure and enjoyment to others always makes us feel good too. So how do you feel about yourself now?

Happy days to all you would-be Father Christmases!

THINK ABOUT IT

What a joy to give with inspiration, fun and love to someone who doesn't expect anything from us at all.

Enjoy fully how this makes you feel in return.

Door N° 17

Make people laugh

This is it! We are now approaching the last full week before Christmas. Still so much to do/buy/achieve? Consequently 'blues' - or sheer panic - might be greatly increased in these last few days before the Midwinter Solstice or Christmas Day. We are all subject to such reactions and stresses. Everyone is in the same boat... more or less. (An unfortunate number of people might feel that they have completely fallen out of the boat and are thrashing around in choppy, inhospitable waters.) But this is the very time that you need to take action to combat the strain of getting it right... doing your best... not letting everyone else down - both for yourself and others around you

So today, I want you to make people laugh - or at least bring a smile to their faces. Tell a joke (even if it makes the listener groan... it's an inverted form of laughter), try a little gentle teasing, act the clown... do a silly walk or dance, cross your eyes or pull funny faces (so long as the wind doesn't change and they stick like that!). Surprise people - even shock them a little - that will also help to loosen their reserve and bring the reaction of laughter to the surface.

Break the tension. Everyone and everything gets so serious and intense, especially at this highly emotionally charged time of year. Just make one person smile and then feel how the whole atmosphere around both of you changes. How do you feel now? Do you also feel different... better... more relaxed... lighter of heart? It's a win/win situation.

If you are staying in at home today, or work on your own, pick up the phone and give someone a call and bring a smile to their lips... a chuckle in their throats... a grin to their face... a belly-laugh to the world.

Remember that laughter is also very beneficial - it promotes good health. It lowers blood sugar levels, boosts the immune system, decreases stress hormones and triggers the release of endorphins - the body's natural feel-good chemicals. Physically it also tones muscles, improves respiration and circulation. Emotionally it unleashes inhibitions, and lowers barriers generating better communication and team building and encourages positive thinking. What an amazing cocktail of wonderful benefits!

Of course, people might think that you have suddenly taken leave of your senses. So what? Who cares? It's nearly Christmas and we all have a lot to be grateful for, to look forward to and to feel jolly about. Yes, we do. Lighten the mood... break the tension. Do it for someone else and you will also feel the benefit.

If you find it difficult to tell jokes or be witty... or just plain daft... try wearing a Christmas hat or pair of silly Christmas spectacles, especially whilst keeping an utterly straight face yourself - and when people begin to notice, pretend that you don't know what they are talking about or reacting to. People will often laugh in sheer surprise, especially if you are the kind of person who doesn't usually do silly things.

The downside is that some people prefer to wilfully remain miserable and can grow increasingly cross the more you try to jolly them along. If you come across someone like that, don't upset them even more, leave them to it. There are plenty more to crack a joke with!

While you are perhaps clowning around and making a real idiot of yourself, also remember that it takes an emotionally balanced and mature person to have the courage to laugh at themselves. You can take some comfort from this fact.

Don't forget to have a good laugh yourself But remember to always laugh with someone, never at them. There is a world of difference.

Seize the day!

THINK ABOUT IT

At this very darkest time of the year go and spread a little metaphorical sunshine!

Happy days!

Door N° 18

Share a living gift

Decide who you might like to give a living plant to this Christmas and make time to visit your local open-air market or garden centre to choose one. Or perhaps you have an abundance of plants already potted up in your own garden? I particularly like to give pots of my scented geraniums as gifts, especially at this, the darkest, dreariest time of year. Fresh green growth and sweetly scented foliage brings a vibrant message of springtime, warmth, optimism and hope.

If you have a garden - or even a small back yard - you might like to plan growing some plants to give as gifts for Christmas. This is really a project for the new year, but you may like to give it a thought now as an antidote to all the other Midwinter thoughts whirling around in your head.

Growing something from seed and watching it develop and flourish can be amazingly satisfying and bring much joy with it too. You needn't tackle anything difficult or complicated. Save your yoghurt and ice cream pots to plant your seeds in - even the cardboard inner tubes from loo rolls can be utilised. Buy a sack of reputable compost that is suitable for seedlings. If recycling plastic pots, clean well and gently punch or burn/melt holes in the bottom of them so that water can drain through.

Fill your pots almost to the top with soil, scatter two or three seeds on the surface and then cover lightly with a sprinkling of more compost. Keep moist but do not over water. March is a good time to plant seeds, so long as the weather isn't too cold. Leave your seed pots outside, somewhere sheltered. Germination can take just five days to several weeks, depending on the type of seed you are growing and the weather.

Once your seedlings have two to four leaves, plant them out into larger pots. Later in the summer you can plant them out into the containers you are going to give them away in, giving the foliage a tidying trim if necessary, allowing for the plants to put out fresh leaves.

Culinary herbs are a perennial favourite and you can group three or four together in a broad-topped pot to make a really attractive and useful display - sage, thyme, oregano and chives are all very easy to grow (but there are lots of others too) and will happily co-exist together. When the time comes to distribute your gifts, clean the outside of the pot by scrubbing it with water and a stiff brush, allow to dry and then tie some brown (compostable) paper around the pot with a broad silk ribbon and there you have the perfect gift, all natural, useful, recyclable.

Just be aware that if you are tempted to re-pot any plants at this time of year, think twice about it... they can catch cold... and certainly never pot anything up (or plant it out, for that matter) if the weather is very cold or frosty. Also bear in mind that some plants may lose their foliage in winter so label clearly what lies beneath the soil and assure the recipient that it will reappear in the springtime.

Whether you grow your own pot plants or buy them, giving the gift of a growing plant is a wonderful thing to do because it changes the whole ambience of any room or area it stands in, just as cut flowers improve and lift the mood and feeling of wherever they are replaced. A growing plant changes the energies around it and helps to bring us into right relation with our natural environment. They can help to re-balance and heal us, which is why we take flowers to a sick person.

However, if you haven't time to organise yourself to give living plants this time around, perhaps you would like to give a loved one the gift of growing something for themselves which is equally as precious. Again, salad, veg or culinary herbs are all relatively easy to grow. Buy one or more packets of seeds, a seed tray or several smaller pots and decant enough potting compost into a smaller bag. Place the compost and packets of seeds attractively into or on top of the pots. Decorate with a seasonal ribbon or silk bow. Hey presto, you have a personal, useful and thoughtful gift! You may also like to include a recipe which uses the plants you have given seeds of - perhaps a family or favourite recipe, typed or written out on paper and tied up with more ribbon in a scroll.

So, I will repeat, take a few moments today to think who you would like to give the gift of living growth to this week, and then have a bit of fun choosing the plant and 'dressing' it ready to present to its new owner. Remember to take some pleasure and fresh living energies from the task yourself. Who said that giving to others couldn't bring its own rewards to the giver too?

Have fun and give pleasure!

THINK ABOUT IT

There are many ways to give the gift of Life.

What better gift could you possibly share?

Life is quintessentially precious - it is what we are all about.

Give freely and joyously.

Door N° 19

Tell someone you love them

As mature, rational adults we are encouraged not to show our deeper feelings, although thankfully this has begun to change over recent years. Many people assume that their nearest and dearest must know that they care, so why state the obvious? But conversely, I would ask why not? We have got very much better at showing our feelings, but not at expressing them verbally.

It is a sad fact that often, if you tell someone you love them, they respond with suspicion: 'Why, what do you want?' or fear, 'Is something wrong?' 'Are you ill?' How dreadful is that? Why should something have to be dire before it is acceptable to express our most dearly held feelings?

Bite the bullet! Today make a point of saying to someone how much you care. For a friend you may wish to tell them how much you appreciate them being in your life, how much you care for them; for a child, parent or partner how much you love them. It is good to clear one's throat and actively, openly speak out. These days we are encouraged to speak our truth, to let the world know how we feel, to not just merely defer to others but to speak up for ourselves, so why not apply the same principles to expressions of care, gratitude, fondness and love?

Unfortunately, we find little or no difficulty in telling others when we are hurt, upset or made angry by them or in criticising them for their shortcomings. So why is it so difficult to share our kinder, more tender feelings? Some people think that showing their finer feelings or speaking out affectionately is a sign of weakness. This couldn't be further from the truth. It takes great courage and strength of character to bare one's soul - to open oneself up to possible rejection or even ridicule. Others make the mistake of thinking that showing anger and belligerent self-righteousness shows how strong and mature one is. Sorry, this simply isn't the case. What they are really demonstrating for all the world to see is that they are easily manipulated, weak, immature and lacking in self-control.

In this modern age of numerous technical devices which all make it so much easier to connect with one another, one of our greatest downfalls is still our bad communication skills. All the devices in the world are not going to solve the problem for us if we still have difficulty actually articulating the words and recognising and acknowledging the sentiments behind them.

It is good to hear these words of affection too. Sounds good in your own ears and certainly sounds good to other people. Have a practice while you are by yourself. Go on. Say 'I love you' out loud... now. And don't forget yourself in all this. Tell yourself how much you really care too. We habitually leave ourselves out and although this 'Alternative Advent Calendar' is focused on what we can give to others in the run up to Christmas, in this instance, telling yourself how much you care is also a gift because we so often ignore ourselves, deprecate ourselves, or at the very least leave ourselves out of any appreciation or consideration.

I shall start the ball rolling. To all of you who are reading this now, I care very deeply about you, even though I might not know who you are, and if you were standing here in front of me now I would give you a great big smile and open my arms to you and give you a great big bear hug. I truly and deeply appreciate all my readers.

Now it's your turn. Be bold. Be definite. Stop beating about the bush. Do it. Make someone's day. Tell those around you just how much you care.

THINK ABOUT IT

Forget yourself.

Think of others.

Give them the gift of hearing that they are cared about.

Provide them with the pleasure of knowing that they are appreciated and loved.

Door N° 20

Extend the hand of friendship

I have already mentioned various aspects of this idea during the course of 'The Alternative Advent Calendar', but I don't think that it can be overstated at any time of the year, let alone at this, the key point, in our annual cycle when giving is so prominently in our thoughts. Midwinter/Christmas is traditionally the season to give of our time, goods, resources and love. We offer selfless acts of hospitality, money, hard work, care and thought more freely at this time of year than at any other.

Traditionally, Midwinter has always been a celebration of peace... An opportunity to lay down one's arms when weaponry was locked away - banned - and even hostile factions could come together - think of the iconic truce between the Germans and the Allied Forces during Christmas, 1914 - they were instinctively following an ancient tradition. Such spontaneous heartfelt flourishing of friendship and care should be encouraged to occur as often and as much as possible and flow over into other seasons, other times of the year. This is indeed a demonstration of the better side of human nature and should be nurtured as much as possible.

We may not now be at actual war (although there are far too many places on the planet that are) but we all experience problems and challenges with people we either do not like for some reason, have had differences of opinion with in the past, or simply do not know, but in our ignorance feel wary or suspicious of.

Today I want you to extend the hand of friendship to one of these people in your life. They are all just regular human beings going about their business, like you; struggling with such challenges as illness, exhaustion, lack of money, difficult jobs, oppressive employers and difficult or worrying relatives. There is enough prejudice and hostility in the world. There is no justification for it. Be the first to activate a change... to initiate something better... to break down the barriers of ignorance, suspicion, resentment and fear.

Yes, there are some people who, for no reason - no fault on their part or yours - you simply cannot take to. That is simply a fact of life. No one is asking you to be best buddies with everyone, but that is also no reason why you shouldn't be courteous, considerate and offer a friendly smile, word or comment whenever you come into contact with them... no reason why you shouldn't be aware if they are in distress and perhaps, just for once, need your company, time and support.

This Midwinter, let your inner light of friendship and care shine out of you. Choose someone you either do not know or do not particularly like. Go out of your way to speak to them kindly... write and personally give to them a Christmas card (doesn't matter if they do not share your religious beliefs - we all understand something kindly and sincerely meant), or find a very simple and inexpensive gift to pass on to them - the gift of light is a really good choice and so appropriate for this time of year, so perhaps a couple of coloured candles tied with a silk ribbon? Simple but useful, appealing and topical. It isn't the item itself, it is what it represents.

What if the distant, unfriendly or grumpy person simply gives a distant, unfriendly or grumpy response? At least you will have tried. It is important not to expect anything back. Just extend your hand of friendship and don't worry if its not returned. Keep blessing them quietly in your heart.

It is common for us to bemoan the state of our twenty-first century world. "What is the world coming to?" is a frequently asked question. "They should do something about it!" 'Who are 'they'? There is no 'they'. There is only you. You can do something to improve the world - your world - today... right now. What is stopping you? Try it.

You never know, in the process you might just discover an absolute gem of a person who becomes a very dear friend.

What have you to lose? But what might you stand to gain in terms of friendship, good will, future co-operation and understanding?

Go on, give it a go!

THINK ABOUT IT

Rise above your doubts of self-worth.

Put aside your self-consciousness.

Extend the hand of friendship and discover how great you truly are.

Door N° 21

Sow Some Seeds

This is the day - the Winter Solstice! In our whole year this is the day of least daylight, (the 'shortest day') and the longest night, or greatest length of darkness. The word 'solstice' comes from the Latin solstitium which means 'sun stands still' and marks the time when the days get neither shorter or longer but appear to pause... until the morning of the 25th December, that is, when the increase in daylight is once more perceptibly measurable by just over one minute and so is looked upon as the day of the birth or re-birth of Light and the Sun/Son.

Today we can definitely turn our faces away from the past year and the recent dark and dreary days towards the new year, the springtime, the lighter, longer, warmer days. This is not to say that the cold, miserable days of winter are over - we have hardly begun with the really bad weather yet! - but it does mean that we have turned the corner. For some time yet the hours of daylight will still be terribly short but the quality of the daylight will have changed; the actual darkness becomes a little less dense and the daylight takes on a brighter quality.

Which is why today - and Christmas morning - are times of great celebration. If you have been following the old Celtic calendar then you might have spent from the end of October (the Celtic new year) metaphorically hibernating; slowing down on all the hustle and bustle of life and seeking quieter, more sedentary occupations... turning within and taking time to re-evaluate all that you have done and all that has happened in your past year. Just as importantly you might have been thinking where you go from here and what you do next.

This is the day to literally begin to put those new plans into action! These are the 'seeds' that I am referring to. Your hopes, dreams, wishes and plans for the coming months. But it is not much use if you are indecisive, unsure, or want to achieve something but are already convinced that it will never really happen. You have to be firm in your intention and very clear about exactly what you do want out of life. You don't have to understand or work out how you might accomplish it, simply know that this is what you want, and this is what you are going to get.

First of all, you have to decide what you want. Next, write each aim, goal or wish very clearly on a small piece of paper and fold it up tightly. Then I want you to literally plant them in the ground -whether that be in a pot of soil, out in your garden, in your local park or on a piece of waste land. Know that your wishes will grow out of the soil with whatever else emerges from the soil into the spring light and warm summer sunshine.

As the daylight fades - or later this evening in the inky darkness - you might like to light one or more candles or tea lights. Place one in the centre to represent and encourage the returning central Sun, then light others to represent each of your wishes for the coming year and place them in a circle around your Sun candle, then sit with them for a little while and contemplate what you have just done.

And for those of you who have planned to give your local birds/wildlife a feast today, don't forget to put it out for them.

May I wish you all a gentle Solstice filled with good thoughts, positive actions and peace.

THINK ABOUT IT

Celebrate the darkness of this day and turn within to find warmth and security.

Celebrate what this darkness represents - the darkest it can get and the fact that the light will now be returning.

Make your intentions definite, positive and firm - decide what you would like to do with these lighter days and work towards making it your reality.

Plant your seeds.

Door N° 22

Offer deep appreciation

Following on from the solar event of the Winter Solstice yesterday, the feeding of the birds or other wildlife and the setting of personal intentions for the coming year, it is a good idea to spend a little time today focusing on the Earth itself.

If the weather permits, step outside for a few minutes. Close your eyes and breathe deeply... yes, even breathing in the fumes of the city, because we have created them - are responsible for them - and they are also a part of our world.

Feel the ground beneath your feet. You are standing on it with all the weight of your body. Really register that there is something solid beneath you, that this is planet Earth which nurtures and supports us in every physical way. Send feelings of deep appreciation down through your body and out of your feet into the ground and deep into the Earth. Where would we be without it? That might sound like a silly question but think about it. This is our land, our place, our planet. And what have we done to it? So, take this opportunity to begin to reverse our thoughtless and ignorant despoiling of this incredible place and replace our rape and ruination of it with some very personal and sincere gratitude and thanks.

Next turn your attention to the air which you are breathing. It may be flawed and polluted, but then again, imperfect as it might be, where would we be without it? Simply focus on the fact that we have an atmosphere to breath and that it gives us life. As you breath in, smell the very essence of the atmosphere. As you breath out, with every exhalation, breath out your appreciation and thanks.

Now pause to consider all the wondrous species of animals, insects, birds and fish which inhabit the globe, in, on and under this earth of ours. All the amazing, bizarre and stunningly beautiful forms of life which breath the same air, eat, sleep and live their own lives along-side us. How privileged we are to co-exist with so much rich and fascinating diversity - and you might also wish to extend this to the human species as well. Actively become aware of sending out your appreciation of all.

Finally, bring your mind to bear on the gorgeously lush mantle of plant life which cloaks our world; which is mind-blowingly beautiful with a staggering ability to survive and thrive... which feeds, protects, shelters and heals us and which also acts as the filter and lungs of the planet and without which we could not breath.

I often hear people say, "Oh, I love to spend time out in nature!" But the natural world surrounds and is close to us all the time, even in our insulated and more sterile home environments, we really cannot get away from it. It is because we have become blind and oblivious to it that we no longer notice it.

We certainly need to strengthen our connection to the natural world. One of the best ways of bringing ourselves into right relation with all levels of life is to begin to practice the art of being kind. It is simple and can be taught to and developed by any age group from tiny children upwards. But it is often neglected for the grander concepts of empathy, compassion and unconditional love - yet out of kindness all these other loftier practices can easily grow.

Send some deep appreciation out from the centre of your chest - from your heart - to all these numerous and stunning life forms. They all play an integral part in the place and survival of the human race. We are all physically made up of earthly molecules and energetic matter; we are all connected to each other by our common source of physical origin.

This concept might make you feel uncomfortably small. Conversely it might succeed in giving you the impression of being a part of something so much greater, so much more amazing, so much more wondrous and beautiful than we could ever be just on our own. Life - ALL life - is truly incredible and, whether we like it or not, we are all a part of it. Surely this is something to celebrate and rejoice in?

THINK ABOUT IT

At least for today, appreciate your natural world around you and acknowledge

with gratitude your place within the whole grand scheme of things.

Door N° 23

Bless your home

It's getting very close to Christmas Day now. There may be chaos in the kitchen, pandemonium in the sitting room, hysteria in the hall and tears in the bedroom... so now is exactly the time to STOP. Stop everything that you are doing and put the kettle on or get out that half-drunk bottle of wine... that box of gorgeous biscuits or chocolates you were keeping... or put some mince pies in the oven to warm. You are going to take a few minutes break.

Sit down, put your feet up.

You may wish to keep this moment of relative calm to yourself - and that is absolutely fine, you owe it to yourself - or you may decide to extend this brief oasis of sanity and peace to the rest of the family or other people resident where you live. If you choose the latter, put on some Christmas music, put more water in the kettle, get more glasses out of the cupboard, sacrifice more biscuits/chocolates/pies or other goodies.

After all, THIS is Christmas. All this work, panic, running about is all a part of our winter celebration. Yes, there are certain chores which need completing, specific things which have to be done. It is not so much what needs doing as your frame of mind while you are doing it which is important. In extreme circumstances, you may have to decide that some things just will not get done. Even with help from others we have to be realistic and admit that we do only have so much energy, time, or money; that perhaps we have been a bit too ambitious this year - or have had other more important activities which have taken our time. So be honest with yourself. Prioritise. Shelve the rest!

We do not have to spend all of these lovely, exciting pre-Christmas days rushing around trying to make everything perfect. Very often we are only doing these things on our own account. Yes, I hate to burst your bubble but you are probably pleasing yourself in attempting to fulfil your own expectations. We have the idea of how our Christmas is going to be and come hell or high water, that is what everyone is going to get. It doesn't have to become a contest. For those things which are an absolute must, see if there is anyone who can give you a hand... or is there something that you can buy instead of bake?

NOW is what is important. It is the accidents, chaos and things that went wrong which tend to cause the most hilarity and stick in the memory long afterwards. So as the kettle comes to the boil, smile and take a deep breath. Sit yourself down with whatever drink you have chosen, put your feet up - literally - close your eyes and simply take in what is around you... the sounds and smells of your home... the decorations which are or aren't yet up, the warmth, the smells of incense, fruit, cooking, perfume, flowers, the wet dog, the sounds of the cat purring, rain beating on the window, music playing, birds chirping outside (have you fed them today?) or perhaps just blessed silence... and stillness.

Can you begin to see and understand how lucky you are, to have what you already have? No matter how imperfect... how incomplete.

If you decide to call your family or friends into the room to share your little respite from all the seasonal hurly-burly, give them this as a gift. Greet them with a smile (no matter how you might have had to crack your face to force it on to your features) and a bright welcome to come and take a break. Give them a warm hug... make a little joke as you hand round the drinks and goodies. Again, think how lucky you are - some people would give everything they have to be able to sit with others as you are doing now.

This is what it is all about. And not just at Christmas, but throughout the year.

Now take that break!

THINK ABOUT IT

What you have to accomplish today is of secondary importance.

It is your frame of mind - your personal outlook - while you are doing it that matters most.

Seize this day and enjoy it to the full.

Door N° 24

Celebrate Mothers' Night

This is it... Christmas Eve and the last door of the Advent Calendar! (However, there is an extra door which I would like you to open tomorrow - Christmas Day - can you guess what might be behind it?)

Today's door is not really about the daytime but about this evening. In many places around the world, but especially in Britain and parts of northern Europe this is when Mother's Night is celebrated. The archetypal 'mother', grandmother' or 'crone' is an ancient feminine figure - in the singular or plural - and predates many of the more recent masculine deities. In Italy there is *Santa Lucia*. In Russia they have *Snegurochke*. In Germany, *Frau Holle* has her sacred work of birthing souls into life on Earth but also birthing souls back out of earthly life onto a higher plain. Centuries ago she became translated into English as Mother Holly while here in Wales we have the goddesses *Modron* and *Rhiannon*.

The 25th December is the day when the solar event of the Solstice is completed and the Sun/Light is reborn. Historically this day has been celebrated as the time of the birth or rebirth of so many solar deities such as Isis, Mithras and Apollo. However, the night before any birth must surely be spent with the mother in labour - as with Mary in the stable before giving birth to Jesus.

However you look at it, this is a sacred time when the feminine aspect within all of us is called upon to birth this annual celebration into our world and nurture those around us. Your task for today - or this evening - is to remember your own mother, or the woman or women who have fulfilled that role for you at different times in your life. If she is still with you on this Earth perhaps you might like to take a few minutes to tell her that you love her and thank her for all she has done for you.

Many of us have serious emotional issues with our mothers but even so, this is the night to try to put all that to one side and think of her with at least a modicum of kindness. Your mother gave birth to you - gave you passage into this world, this life. She is only a humble, ordinary human being, full of flaws and challenges. Be kind to her, if only in your thoughts.

Conversely, if you are a mother or parent yourself, you might wish to gather your children about you and let them know how much you love them - or if they are not with you, then pick up the phone and call them. At the same time, do not forget to honour that of the Mother and that aspect of a tender, nurturing nature within yourself - whether you be male or female - we all have a feminine side to our nature.

This evening, when all the last-minute preparations have been seen to and the rest of the family has bustled away to finish wrapping their gifts or flake out in front of the television or whatever it is they need to do, find a quiet corner for yourself. Light a single candle and pour yourself a glass of good wine - or make yourself a hot non-alcoholic drink or sparklingly chilled fruit cup if you prefer. Sit quietly and think about this sacred feminine role which so many of us seek, to some degree, to fulfil... or sometimes totally avoid. How do you demonstrate your feminine aspects? How have you seen others demonstrate theirs? What is so especially important about them? Why do we thrive surrounded by feminine care and attention and crave it and suffer if it is missing from our life?

Acknowledge and celebrate the mother(s) in your life, including your own mothering capabilities, and also remember the greatest mother figure we have which is the Earth herself. Be gentle in your evaluation and reflection.

My greatest respect to all of you who are fulfilling the role of 'mother' tonight.

THINK ABOUT IT

Be gently thankful for all of the people in your life who demonstrate an element of kindly nurture and care towards you.

Be tolerant and understanding of those who are so challenged and lost to themselves that they find it painful or difficult to do so.

Recognise your own nurturing abilities and be thankful for them; encourage them to increase and prosper with you.

Door N° 25

The extra door

These days, modern advent calendars usually only have 24 doors, ending on Christmas Eve. But as the Merry Midwinter calendar has in no way resembled an ordinary advent calendar so far, I thought that an extra door would be appropriate.

This is a door which I want you to open literally. It is the door to your home... your own front door. Step outside it. Take some deep breaths. If anyone is walking past, smile and call a seasonal greeting to them. If anyone is driving past, smile and give them a cheery wave. Look around you. Notice the buildings, the trees, the plants, birds and animals. Know that you are connected to them all. Know, too, that in some measure you are also responsible for them all. They are a part of you and you are a part of them. Nothing is isolated or separate in this world - this is an illusion which humanity has built up around itself out of fear or a feeling of superiority. Give to ALL your appreciation and thanks on this very special and blessed day.

Think back over some of the things which you have done this past twenty-four days. Did you find them easy... difficult... challenging... satisfying... heart-warming, ...distressing... enjoyable? What do you think the effects of your endeavours might have been? Was it worth it? (Although you can never really tell exactly what effect your actions may have had on others.) How do you feel about your Advent activities now? How have they made you feel?

It was suggested that you did these little acts of thoughtfulness and kindness for the community around you in the run up to our very special Midwinter celebrations to help you get into the spirit of things.

But why stop doing this sort of thing now, just because we have reached the 25th December? Does the passing of a certain date mean that we can forget to be kind, to take care, to be involved and actively concerned, to show our love?

How often do we hear the questions asked: "Why can't it be like this all year round? Why can't people behave like this all the time?" The simple answer is that they can. Life can be so much more friendly, positive, understanding, tolerant and happy. But don't wait for everyone else to start behaving differently. The change begins with you. What are you going to do?

Along the way you will have garnered lots of new or different experiences, many memories, possibly new friends or renewed friendships, laughter, satisfaction, a different perspective on your life, a new awareness of the natural world, and much, much more. These are the invisible gifts which lay hidden, waiting for you within the advent doors. You were tasked - challenged - to do something for the people, animals, wildlife and places around you. But, hopefully, carrying out each action will have given you intangible but everlasting rewards.

When you return inside, I would like you to open another door... an extremely special and unique door - the door to your heart.

TRUE CHRISTMAS IS A STATE OF MIND
AND A WAY OF LIFE...

ALL YEAR ROUND!

A very merry Christmas to you all, with my love.

What happens after Christmas?

Once Christmas and New Year has passed, many of us often feel a huge sense of anti-climax and disappointment. January seems to loom as a dull, flat, drab and pointless month with little or nothing to look forward to.

Why not bring fresh focus and inspiration into your life and the lives of everyone around you? If you received this little book as a gift for Christmas - in other words, once Advent had actually passed - why not follow it through January instead? Few of the suggestions behind the Doors are specifically related to Christmas, but for those that are, I have provided some alternative ideas, to use on these days or during the added number of days in the month... or to use at other times of the year. I am sure that you can also think of your own activities and there is extra space in which to jot down your self-challenging ideas.

These activities can apply to any time of the year, any season You might even decide to follow it every month - at least in some respects. Why not? Let your endeavours to create a better life around yourself have free rein throughout the length of the whole year.

ALTERNATIVE SUGGESTIONS TO SEASONALLY RELATED CHALLENGES:

☼ It doesn't have to be Saint Nicholas' Day to perform kind and thoughtful actions and acknowledgements - you can give the gift of a genuine complement any day of the year.

☼ It doesn't have to be Advent or Christmas to sing, hum or whistle any song or piece of music. Bring enthusiasm into your world and open your throat to make joyful sounds - even if it isn't as melodious as you might wish. No one says that you have to give a performance in front of others. Wait until you are alone and then let rip!

☼ It doesn't have to be Christmas to give you a reason to write a card, notelet or message to someone. Drop a friendly line, if only to wish someone a wonderful spring, a happy Bank Holiday weekend, a lovely Midsummer, autumn equinox or harvest season. Buy a postcard of your local town or tourist attraction and simply tell them that you are thinking of them. It is always heart-warming to know that you are in someone's thoughts besides which, having an envelope - other than 'bumf' and bills - descend onto one's doormat is always a treat.

☼ Instead of surprising someone totally unsuspecting with the gift of a Christmas stocking, why not bake some biscuits, flapjacks or fairy cakes? Pack a few in a clear plastic bag (so that they can see that you aren't actually giving them something offensive) and tie with a colourful ribbon. If you decide to present it to someone you don't really know - like a check-out assistant at the supermarket or a car park attendant - all you need to say is something like "You've always been so pleasant/friendly/helpful - I just wanted to say 'thank you'".

NOTE: In this age when so many people are suffering from food allergies, it might be a good idea to include a list of all the ingredients so that the recipient knows if it is safe for them to eat.

SUGGESTED CHALLENGES FOR OTHER DAYS

☼ Give something back to your local area.

☼ Pick up litter - but always remember to wear rubber gloves whilst you do so.

☼ Sow wildflower seeds on waste ground or roadside verges, but always check first what wild-flower seeds you have got and if they are appropriate for your area.

☼ Invite someone in for a coffee or a glass of wine.

☼ Volunteer for charity work - there are also charitable activities that you can engage in at home, like knitting blanket squares, sewing dresses for little girls in hot countries or knitting teddies for injured and traumatised refugee children to comfort and assist in their recovery.

☼ Offer praise of someone else's garden - everyone needs a little encouragement and one's garden is such a personal thing, yet on show for the whole world to see.

☼ Offer to help someone else with a task in their garden.

☼ If you do some baking, offer a piece or slice to a neighbour - they don't have to be elderly - we all welcome a lift to our day that an unexpected treat can bring.

☼ Offer to sit with a neighbour while their carer takes a break.

☼ Offer to baby-sit - give parents a break, especially if they haven't got extended family living near-by.

☼ Say 'thank you' - to anyone and everyone around you who are working for and in your community - and this means council workmen, the police, shop assistants, builders, bank clerks, waitresses... everyone. 'Without what they do, your local community wouldn't be half so easy or attractive to live in. Also, in our modern society it is unfortunate that many people do not earn good wages, no matter how hard they work. Even if they are well paid, it is still lovely to be seen and acknowledged for what one does.

☼ Open your door to all. Invite all your neighbours to supper - and I mean ALL your neighbours... as many as you can sensibly fit inside your house. Ask everyone to bring something to eat, pool their offerings and see what a splendid meal everyone assembles.

MORE IDEAS? MAKE A NOTE OF THEM HERE:

This space below is for you to fill in your own ideas of how you might serve, enrich or assist your community:

Acknowledgements

First and foremost, I would like to thank my son, Dafydd, who has tirelessly supported, encouraged, offered positive criticism and finally formatted and readied 'The Alternative Advent Calendar' for publication. I am also indebted to my editor, Jessica Thiele for all her hard work and gentle patience on my behalf.

I would like to particularly mention my dearest friend, Alison Weetman, who has given me so many loving suggestions as to how I could clarify some of the content of my manuscript.

Many people have provided me with inspiration and encouragement - friends, family and enthusiastic readers of my work for which I am truly appreciative and thankful.

I would also like to thank my dear husband, Holger for his uncomplaining and generous support... for all the meals and cups of tea he has unstintingly provided me with... for all the time and space he has created for me in which to write and work unhindered.

It is always said that the life of a writer is a lonely, solitary one, and in many respects it is. But none of us achieves anything completely alone. We all interdepend on many others, even if they are as obscure and distant as the people who supply our electricity with which to light our lamps and power our heating systems, the folk who have fashioned our pens and paper or manufactured our computers, the farmers who have grown the tea and coffee for that all-important revitalising cuppa... and so it goes on. So, lastly, to all the many invisible people who have also enabled me to work and produce this book, I thank you all with deep gratitude and appreciation.

About the Author

Gillian Monks is a Quaker, Theosophist and practising Druid. She was born and brought up in Lancashire and trained as a teacher, graduating from Lancaster University. Gillian is developing a spiritual retreat on a five-acre plot where she also leads and facilitates workshops in self-development and spirituality. She lives with her husband and son, five cats and two dogs in the heart of Snowdonia. This is Gillian's second book, her first being 'Merry Midwinter; How to Rediscover the Magic of the Christmas Season' which was published by Unbound in 2018.

Read More About Gillian

www.gillianmonks.com

www.ingramcontent.com/pod-product-compliance
Lightning Source LLC
Chambersburg PA
CBHW030329080526
44584CB00012B/782